D1474464

Like Mother, Like Daughter

Two Generations of Quilts

BY KAREN WITT AND ERIN WITT

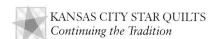

KANSAS CITY STAR QUILTS
Continuing the Tradition

Like Mother, Like Daughter:
Two Generations of Quilts
By Karen Witt and Erin Witt

Editor: Kimber Mitchell
Designer: Amy Robertson
Photography: Aaron T. Leimkuehler
Illustration: Eric Sears
Technical Editor: Nan Doljac
Production assistance: Jo Ann Groves

Published by:
Kansas City Star Books
1729 Grand Blvd.
Kansas City, Missouri, USA 64108

First edition, first printing
ISBN: 978-1-935362-47-0

Library of Congress Control Number: 2010927145

Printed in the United States of America
By Walsworth Publishing Co., Marceline, MO

Dedication

We dedicate this book to our loving husband and father, Joe Witt, who has spent his entire married life dodging loose threads and straight pins. He has helped us move boxes and boxes of fabric, stuffed thousands of quilt patterns into plastic sleeves, cut fabric for kits and shows, driven endless miles to pick up supplies and make deliveries, eaten around piles of quilting paraphernalia on the kitchen table, and always encouraged us in all our endeavors.

Acknowledgments

What a wonderful new adventure it has been to write a book together. Our grateful thanks go to:

• **Diane McLendon** and **Doug Weaver** of Kansas City Star Books for making this book possible.

• The creative team at Kansas City Star Books—our designer, **Amy Robertson**; technical editor, **Nan Doljac**; and illustrator, **Eric Sears**.

• Our talented photographer, **Aaron T. Leimkuehler**. He sprinkled "pixie dust" over each of our vignettes and helped the location shots, which were photographed in Lexington and Winchester, KY, turn out exactly as we had envisioned.

• A special thanks to our editor, **Kimber Mitchell**, who walked us through each step of the publishing process.

• **Hugh James** of Lexington Furniture Co. in Lexington, KY, for allowing us to photograph some of Erin's quilts in his beautiful store.

• **Cindy Ford** for the opportunity to photograph one of Karen's quilts in her perfectly restored home, built between 1810 and 1814.

• And finally, this book would not have been possible without some helpful "elves"—special quilting friends who encouraged us, proofread patterns, and stitched and long-arm quilted some of the projects in this book. Without the friendship and support of others who enjoy the art of quilting as much as we do, life would be quite dull and lonely!

Contents

About the Authors

— ⚜ —

Karen Witt was practically born with a needle in her hand. In fact, her mother once told her that her first thought upon seeing her newborn daughter was what a small thimble she would need! She started sewing at the machine when she was just four, helping her mother stitch together scraps to make crocheted rag rugs. Later childhood sewing projects included doll clothes and aprons. Before long, Karen was sewing her own clothing. Her sewing repertoire eventually expanded to other needlework skills such as cross stitch, knitting, embroidery, needlepoint, and crochet. In college, she majored in Home Economics.

While Karen always enjoyed sewing and needlework, she knew she'd found her true passion when she discovered quilting in the mid 1970s. By 1985, she decided to forgo all her other crafts to concentrate on quilting. She eventually began teaching quilting classes and designing her own quilts. In 2005, Karen started her own company, Reproduction Quilts, attending her first Quilt Market with 12 original patterns inspired by 19TH-century antique quilts. The patterns were soon picked up by national distributors and sold to quilt shops across the country. Karen's quilts have been published in numerous national and international quilt magazines, and several have won awards at national quilt shows, including the American Quilter's Society and the National Quilting Association. She lives in Winchester, Kentucky, with her husband, Joe.

Erin Witt was born into a home where threads and pins were always on the floor and quilting projects always in progress. In a family that includes five generations of needlework enthusiasts, she has been an avid quilter for as long as she can remember. She stitched her first quilt at the tender age of only three. And as a youngster, she loved to sew, cross stitch, and knit. Erin earned her undergraduate degree in Textiles and Merchandising from Eastern Kentucky University and is pursuing a Master of Science degree in Merchandising, Apparel, and Textiles from the University of Kentucky.

In 2006, Erin joined Karen at Reproduction Quilts and the two share an office as well as travel together as teachers and quilt show vendors. In 2008, she launched her own quilt design business—Erin Witt Designs—and she currently divides her time between the two companies. She believes quilting can be fun at all ages and particularly enjoys working with beginning and intermediate quilters. Erin lives in Lexington, Kentucky.

Left: Erin and her golden retriever, Scarlett; bottom right: Karen.

Introduction

For the past five years, we've been blessed to work side-by-side in the quilting industry, designing and creating quilts as well as traveling across the country and even to France to teach classes and lecture. While we share a passion for quilting, our designs take decidedly different paths. Karen loves designing classic quilts inspired by antique examples and frequently works with 1800s reproduction fabrics. She enjoys each step of the quilting process—from fabric selection to pattern design to construction, even binding—and is happiest when working leisurely at her sewing machine or with a quilt and needle in hand. Erin, on the other hand, loves the simple yet sophisticated flair of contemporary designs and enjoys creating manageable projects that come together quickly. The term "UFO" isn't in her vocabulary as she can't imagine waiting months—let alone years—to enjoy her new creations!

This book is a reflection of our shared love of quilting as well as our own unique approaches to the craft. The premise for it all began when Erin saw a traditional basket block that Karen was sewing. While she liked it, her creative mind couldn't help but ponder what it might look like without the basket handles. Acting on that thought, she designed her own handle-less basket block—which became the centerpiece for her Home for the Holidays quilt, featured in this book. That creative ingenuity, in turn, sparked an even bigger idea for us— What if we each challenged ourselves to create our own unique versions of a series of themed quilt projects? And with that challenge in mind, our idea for this book came

to fruition. We each designed and created our own renditions of five quilt themes—pieced baskets, quilts made from one block design, quick quilts with a twist, appliqué quilts, and multi-sided designs such as hexagons and snowball blocks. While our projects are based on the same concept, they couldn't be more different in style. But isn't that part of the fun of quilting?

This book also includes our handy guide to labeling your quilts. It is important to take that extra step in the quiltmaking process so that future generations will know the history behind your quilts. How often have you seen an antique quilt and wished it could talk, revealing the maker and when it was made? To make the task easier, we've included a host of tips for creating your own fun labels, including three essential pieces of information that every quilt label should have. So please join us on this fun quilting adventure. Whether your own quilting style takes a traditional or contemporary path, we hope you'll find a project—or more—that you won't be able to resist making!

Karen   Erin

Clockwise from top right: Young Erin with mom, Karen, and brother, Joshua. Middle: Karen and Erin at International Quilt Festival in Houston. Bottom left: Erin sewing a skirt at age 8. Bottom right: Erin learning to crochet from her great grandmother

Pieced Baskets

Whether they're appliquéd or pieced, baskets are a favorite motif among quilters and we are no exception. For our basket challenge, we took a typical basket block but gave it two distinct looks by changing a simple design element and the color palette. Inspired by the scrappy quilts of the 1800s when women made do with what they had, Karen created her version with a wide array of reproduction fabrics—thanks to her large stash of 1800s repro fabrics. For visual interest, she set the pieced blocks on point, which also provided a place to spotlight more detailed quilting in the setting triangles.

Erin wanted to create a Christmas-themed quilt to decorate her home during the holidays. As a younger quilter without a stash, she shopped for a large-scale theme fabric and added three coordinating prints. She decided to remove the basket handles for her design, shifting the look of her quilt from traditional to contemporary. In a clever twist, she combined the basket block with a single central pieced block and completed the quilt with complementary pieced setting and corner triangles.

Scrappy Baskets

Designed by Karen Witt • Finished quilt size: 85" x 102" • Finished block size: 14"

Quilters of the 1800s often looked to their surroundings for design inspiration, and baskets—a common element of daily life—were a popular quilt theme. This block, which features four baskets with pointed handles, reflects my vision of a late 19th-century basket quilt. It is the perfect project for using up your fat quarters or leftover scraps of reproduction fabrics. To unify the medley of scraps, I added a traditional border of Flying Geese units. Following the lead of antique quilts, this quilt has only three borders. In the 19th century, quilters would not have wasted time making a top border because it would not have been visible underneath the pillows.

FABRIC REQUIREMENTS

Baskets and basket backgrounds:

- 2½ yards assorted medium/dark prints OR one scrap of 6" x 10" of 72 different medium/dark prints for baskets
- 2½ yards light prints for basket backgrounds

Border Flying Geese units, basket block rectangles, and binding:

- 2⅔ yards small green print

Basket block square centers and border Flying Geese units:

- 1¼ yards small red print

Setting triangles and corner triangles:

- 2¼ yards beige print

Sashing:

- 3 yards border print

CUTTING INSTRUCTIONS

All measurements include a ¼" seam allowance.

For each 14" finished basket block, select four medium/dark print fabrics and from each fabric, cut:

- 1—4⅞" square from a medium/dark print. Then cut in half once diagonally to make "A" triangles (You will have one extra triangle).
- 1—2⅞" square from a medium/dark print. Then cut in half once diagonally to make 2 "C" triangles.
- 2—1" x 5" strips for "D" basket handles.

For each 14" basket block, select one light fabric and from each fabric, cut:

- 2—4⅞" squares. Then cut each square in half once diagonally to make 4 "A" triangles.
- 8—2½" "B" squares.
- 2—3⅞" squares. Then cut each square in half once diagonally to make 4 "E" triangles.

For joining basket blocks, cut:

- 72—2½" x 6½" strips from small green print.
- 18—2½" squares for block centers from small red print.

For sashing, cut:

- 24—3" x 14½" length of fabric strips from border print.
- 2—3" x 19½" length of fabric strips from border print.
- 2—3" x 52½" length of fabric strips from border print.
- 2—3" x 85½" length of fabric strips from border print.
- 1—3" x 102" length of fabric strip from border print.

For border Flying Geese units, cut:

- 84—4" squares from small green print. Then cut each square in half once diagonally to make a total of 168 triangles.
- 21—7¼" squares from small red print. Then cut each square in half twice diagonally to make a total of 84 triangles.

Scrappy Baskets

For bottom border only, cut:
- 1—6½" x 13½" rectangle from small green print for 1889 appliqué background.
- Appliqué templates on page 17.

For binding, cut:
- 10—2¼" strips the width of fabric from small green print. Then piece strips together end to end.

For setting triangles, cut:
- 3—24" squares from beige print. Then cut each square in half twice diagonally to make 10 triangles (you will have 2 extra triangles).

For corner triangles, cut:
- 2—12¾" squares. Cut each square in half once diagonally to make 4 triangles.

SEWING INSTRUCTIONS

Use a ¼" seam allowance and sew all pieces with right sides together. Press seams toward the darker fabric.

Basket blocks
- Each 14" finished block features 4 baskets—each a different color. All four basket units use the same lighter background print.

1. Sew one medium/dark print "A" triangle to one light print "A" triangle.

2. Sew one light print "B" square to one medium/dark print "C" triangle.

3. Sew one 1" x 5" "D" strip to each side of an "E" triangle. Then trim the excess portions of the "D" strip.

4. Assemble the units constructed in Steps 1–3 to make a 6½" x 6½" basket block.

5. Select three different fabrics for baskets and repeat Steps 1-4 for each to make a total of 4—6½" x 6½" basket blocks.

6. Sew two 6½" x 6½" basket blocks to opposite sides of one 2½" x 6½" small green print rectangle. Make a total of two of these rows.

7. Sew two 2½" x 6½" small green print rectangles to opposite sides of one 2½" small red print square.

8. Combine the three rows made in Steps 6 and 7 to create a 14½" block.

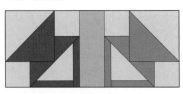

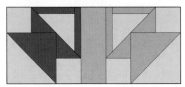

9. Repeat Steps 6-8 to make a total of 18—14" finished basket blocks.

Scrappy Baskets

BORDER
Flying Geese units

1. Sew 1 small green print triangle to each side of a large red small print triangle to make a 3½" x 6½" Flying Geese unit. Repeat to make a total of 84 Flying Geese units.

2. Referring to the diagram below, sew 32 Flying Geese units together for the two side borders.

3. Referring to the next diagram, sew 10 Flying Geese units together. Repeat to make a second strip.
4. Using the French Script lettering on page 17, appliqué the year "1889" on a 6½" x 13½" small green print rectangle. If you prefer, you can appliqué your initials instead of the date.
5. Sew the two Flying Geese unit strips from Step 3 to opposite sides of the 6½" x 13½" appliquéd rectangle.

TIP: Many quilts from as early as 1850 have initials and/or dates on the front. Sometimes these details or even the full name of the maker were discretely quilted into the project as a permanent label. Other quilters made a bolder statement by appliquéing large numbers and letters that proclaimed the year the quilt was made or the maker's name.

Working With Border Prints

Border prints—designs that are printed specifically to be cut into strips—add style and period charm to your quilts. They're authentic to the antique quilts of the early 1800s, which featured them in medallion frames, sashing, and borders. When selecting a border print for the sashing in this quilt, look for one that has repeating stripes that will finish 2½" in width. You may need more fabric than usual. You will need at least ½" between the strips for seam allowance.

An Enduring Tradition

The golden age of quilting—the mid 1800s—was over by the time a quilt such as Scrappy Baskets would have been made. After the Civil War, America experienced tremendous industrial growth and with it, stores began carrying manufactured bedding and city dwellers began replacing the quilts on their beds with store-bought bedcoverings. Even those who lived in rural areas—typically the more affluent—would order their bedding from companies such as Sears and Roebuck or Montgomery Ward. But despite the trend toward manufactured goods, quilting continued to flourish particularly on the frontier and in rural areas.

Quilts in the style of Scrappy Baskets represented the workmanship of women who enjoyed handwork and often used their needlework to decorate their homes. State quilt documentation books are filled with scrappy quilts made of fabrics spanning several decades. My quilt contains numerous small prints indicative of those that would have been available from about 1825 to the late 1800s. The sashing fabric in Scrappy Baskets is patterned after an early 1800s print. Such a quilt would have merited special quilting, so the maker most likely would have showcased her skills through a variety of curved lines and elegant motifs—often found in mid 19th-century quilts.

SASHING AND QUILT CENTER

1. Sew a 3" x 14½" border print sashing strip to the bottom of each 14½" basket block.
2. Referring to the assembly diagram below, lay out the blocks, remaining sashing strips, setting triangles, and corner triangles. Then sew the segments into rows.
3. Referring to the assembly diagram, sew the rows together.
4. Press and trim the quilt center, which should measure 73½" x 96½".

5. Referring to the assembly diagram, sew the bottom border to the quilt center.
6. Referring to the assembly diagram, sew the side borders to the quilt center.

Quilt, then bind. To replicate the narrow rolled-edge finish of antique quilts, trim the quilt about ⅜" from the stitching line and firmly roll the binding over to the back of the quilt. As a result, more of the binding will show on the back than the front.

1889

Assembly Diagram

Scrappy Baskets

How To Make A Scrappy Quilt

As quilters, we tend to find ourselves collecting fabrics, sometimes without any specific plan for using them. When making 19th-century style quilts, it is helpful to learn how to identify the approximate time periods represented in reproduction fabrics so you can create quilts that accurately reflect the era you want to capture. State documentation books and quilt history books are great resources for this task. If making a reproduction 1820s quilt, the fabric choices are somewhat limited. However, if making a circa 1889 quilt such as Scrappy Baskets, you'll have a wider array of material to choose from because quilts of that time period used fabrics ranging from early 1800s wood block prints, toiles, and Turkey reds to later chromes, purples, shirtings, and madders.

As you plan a scrappy quilt, first select a theme fabric such as a large-scale floral print to establish the quilt's color scheme and create visual continuity throughout the quilt. That sense of harmony seems intrinsic to our 21st-century quilting sensibilities. My Scrappy Baskets seemed to call for a multicolored border print in the sashing strips, which unifies the many basket colors. Next, it is important to select a variety of fabrics that vary in value and scale. Value is the difference between lightness and darkness and is determined by the fabrics surrounding the selected fabric. The amount of contrast you choose is a personal matter. However, most antique quilts seem to have low or muted levels of contrast—an important detail to keep in mind if you want to make an authentic reproduction.

Scale is the size of the motif printed on the fabric. Although the baskets in my quilt are small, I did incorporate some large-scale prints. Chintzes and paisleys, for example, are wonderful large-scale reproduction fabrics. Every scrappy quilt needs some plaids and linear designs such as stripes. These fabrics transcend the decades and add authenticity to your quilt. Round out your fabric selection with some medium-scale prints (1" or larger motifs) and small prints.

Fussy cutting fabrics can also add period-appropriate character to your quilts. Nineteenth-century quilters loved to fussy cut as much as today's quilters. But be careful to balance fussy-cut blocks with pieced ones to avoid an overly contrived look. If you have a favorite fabric but not enough of it to cut in one piece, simply piece two scraps together and cut the template from the patched area. That's exactly what our quilting ancestors did!

As you select your fabrics, keep in mind that 19th-century quilters did not stress about color combinations as much as today's quilters do. They simply used what they had. So if you have a large chintz and want a coordinating small print, you don't have to choose one in the exact same shade. Instead, look for a fabric that blends with rather than matches the large chintz, or use a fabric in a complementary color. There are 72 baskets in this quilt, so try stepping outside of your color comfort zone for some of them. The goal is to have a quilt that sparks visual interest rather than one that's perfectly balanced. There is a lot of visual energy in this quilt, so a block "with an attitude" here or there will only add interest to the overall design.

After you've finished making half of the blocks, lay them out on a design wall, floor, or bed. Then stand back and take a photo. What do you see? Is there a variety of colors as well as values? If not, decide what is needed to enhance the overall composition. And last but not least, incorporate an area in your quilt where the eye can rest. Because scrappy quilts have lots of visual activity by nature, that calming element is important. In Scrappy Baskets, the soft green and muted red found in each block as well as the Flying Geese border unify the quilt's color palette.

A B C D E F G
H I J K L M N
N O P Q R S T
U V W X Y Z
1 2 3 4 5 6 7 8 9 0

For date on Scrappy Baskets, enlarge numbers 320%, then enlarge that size 200%.

For initials on Scrappy Baskets, enlarge letters 230%, then enlarge that size 200%.

Home for the Holidays

Designed by Erin Witt • Finished quilt size: 60" x 60" • Finished block size: 14" x 14"

— ⚜ —

Christmas is my favorite time of year, and I must admit to getting a little carried away with the spirit of the season. I slip into elf mode right after Thanksgiving and begin decorating, cooking, shopping, singing, and sewing. This quilt was inspired by what I call my Charlie Brown Christmas tree—a sparse little tree I purchased while a college student. During the holidays, it sets atop a table in my TV room where its twinkling lights remind me of so many wonderful memories. Once the holidays are over, you can easily use the quilt as a festive wall hanging, table topper, or couch throw throughout the rest of the year.

FABRIC REQUIREMENTS

Basket blocks, central block, setting triangles, corner triangles, and inner border:

- 1¼ yard green print
- 1 yard cream tonal
- 1⅝ yards red tonal

Sashing and outer border:

- 1⅞ yards red large floral

Tree Skirt

It's easy to convert this festive quilt into a tree skirt by simply cutting an 8-inch circle in its center and binding the resulting raw edges. A tree will easily slip into the opening. And by cutting only a small circle instead of the traditional slit from the middle all the way to the edge, the quilt can be used as a table topper after the holidays by placing a punch bowl or centerpiece over the hole.

CUTTING INSTRUCTIONS

All measurements include a ¼" seam allowance.

For the basket blocks (Block A), cut:

- 8—4⅞" squares from green print. Cut each square in half once diagonally to make 16 large triangles.
- 16—2½" x 6½" rectangles from green print.
- 8—2½" x 4½" rectangles from green print.
- 16—2½" squares from green print.
- 16—2⅞" squares from cream tonal. Cut each square in half once diagonally to make 32 small triangles.
- 16—2½" squares from cream tonal.
- 8—4⅞" squares from red tonal. Cut each square in half once diagonally to make 16 large triangles.
- 16—2⅞" squares from red tonal. Cut each square in half once diagonally to make 32 small triangles.
- 4—2½" squares from red tonal.

For Block B, cut:

- 1—4½" square from large red floral.
- 4—3" x 4½" rectangles from cream tonal.
- 4—3" x 4½" rectangles from green print.
- 4—4⅛" squares from cream tonal.
- 4—3⅜" squares from green print. Then cut each square in half once diagonally to make 8 triangles.
- 8—3⅜" squares from cream tonal. Cut each square in half once diagonally to make 16 triangles.

For setting and corner triangles, cut:
- 4—4½" squares from red tonal.
- 12—3" x 4½" rectangles from cream tonal.
- 12—3" x 4½" rectangles from green print.
- 16—4⅛" squares from cream tonal.
- 8—3⅜" squares from green print. Then cut each square in half once diagonally to make 16 triangles.
- 16—3⅜" squares from cream tonal. Then cut in half once diagonally to make 32 triangles.

For sashing, cut:
- 16—2½" x 14½" strips from red large floral.
- 12—2½" squares from red tonal for square keystones.

For inner border, cut:
To ensure accurate border strips, wait to cut them until after the quilt center is made and measured.
- 2—2½" x 45¾" strips from red tonal.
- 2—2½" x 49¾" strips from red tonal.

For outer border, cut:
To ensure accurate border strips, wait to cut them until after the quilt center is made and measured.
- 2—5¾" x 49¾" strips from red large floral.
- 2—5¾" x 60¼" strips from red large floral.

For binding, cut:
- 6—2½" strips the width of fabric from red tonal. Then piece strips together end to end.

SEWING INSTRUCTIONS
Use a ¼" seam allowance and sew pieces right sides together. Press seams toward the darker fabric.

Block A
1. Sew 1 small cream tonal triangle to 1 small red tonal triangle to create a 2½" half-square triangle unit. Repeat to make a total of 16 units.

2. Sew 1 large red tonal triangle to 1 large green print triangle to create a 4½" half-square triangle unit. Repeat to make a total of 16 units.

3. Sew two cream/red half-square triangle units to opposite sides of a 2½" green print square. Repeat to make a total of 8 of these rows.

4. Sew a 2½" x 6½" green print rectangle to the top of the unit created in Step 3. Repeat to make a total of 8 of these units.

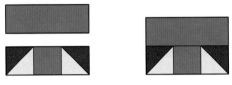

5. Sew two of the large 4½" red/green half-square triangle units created in Step 2 to opposite sides of one unit created in Step 4. Repeat to make a total of 8 of these rows.

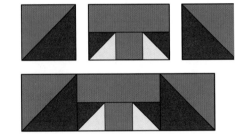

6. Sew a cream tonal triangle to a red tonal triangle to create a 2½" half-square triangle unit. Repeat to make a total of 16 units.

7. Sew a 2½" cream/red print half-square triangle unit to a 2½" cream print square. Repeat to make a total of 16 units (Referring to diagram in Step 8, please note that 8 of the units should have the half-square triangle unit to the left of the cream print square and 8 of the units should have the half-square triangle unit to the right of the cream print square).

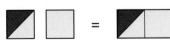

Home for the Holidays

8. Sew two of the units created in Step 7 to opposite sides of a 2½" green print square. Repeat to make a total of 8 of these rows.

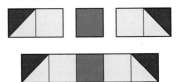

9. Sew two 2½" x 4½" green print rectangles to opposite sides of a 2½" red tonal square. Repeat to make a total of 4 of these rows.

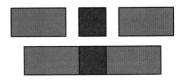

10. Sew two rows created in Step 8 to the top and bottom of one row created in Step 9. Repeat to make a total of 4 of these units.

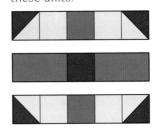
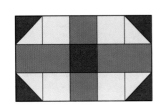

11. Sew two 2½" x 6½" green print rectangles to opposite sides of the units created in Step 10 to make a total of 4 of these units.

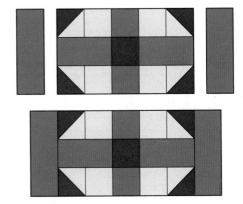

12. Sew two of the rows created in Step 5 to the top and bottom of the row created in Step 11. This completes Block A. Repeat to make a total of 4 basket blocks.

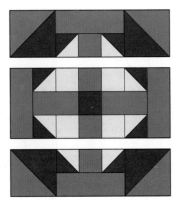
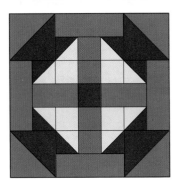

Block B

1. Sew 2 large cream tonal triangles and 2 large green print triangles to opposite sides of a 4⅛" cream tonal square to make a 5½" square-in-a-square unit. Repeat to make 4 of these units.

 =

2. Sew one 3" x 4½" cream print rectangle to one 3" x 4½" green print rectangle. Repeat to make 4 units.

3. Sew two of the square-in-square units created in Step 1 to opposite ends of one pieced unit created in Step 2. Repeat to make a total of 2 of these rows.

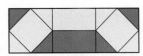

4. Sew two pieced square units made in Step 2 to opposite sides of a 4½" red tonal square.

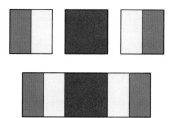

5. Sew the two rows created in Step 3 to the top and bottom of the row created in Step 4. This completes Block B.

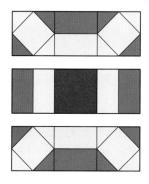

Setting triangles

1. Sew 2 cream tonal triangles to opposite sides of a 4⅛" cream tonal square. Sew one green print triangle to another side of the 4⅛" cream tonal square. Repeat to make a total of 8 units.

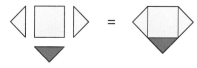

2. Sew 2 cream tonal triangles and two green triangles to opposite sides of a 4⅛" cream tonal square to make one square-in-a-square unit. Repeat to make a total of 4 units.

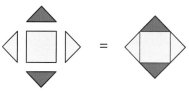

3. Sew one 3" x 4½" cream print rectangle to one 3" x 4½" green print rectangle. Repeat to make 8 units. The finished unit should be 4½" x 5½".

4. Sew one unit created in Step 1 to the left of the pieced unit created in Step 3. Sew one square-in-a-square unit created in Step 2 to the right side of the pieced unit. Repeat to make a total of 4 of these rows.

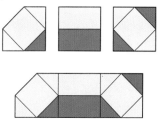

5. Sew a pieced unit from Step 3 to the right side of a 4½" red tonal square. Repeat to make a total of 4 of these rows.

6. Referring to the diagram below, combine the units created in Steps 1, 4 and 5. Repeat to make a total of 4 setting triangles.

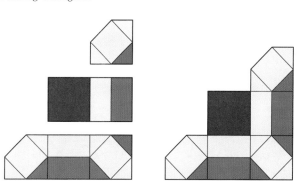

Corner triangles

1. Sew two cream tonal triangles to opposite sides of a 4⅛" cream tonal square. Then sew a green print triangle to another side of the 4⅛" cream tonal square. Repeat to make 8 units.

2. Sew one 3" x 4½" cream print rectangle to one 3" x 4½" green print rectangle. Repeat to make 4 units.

3. Sew two of the units created in Step 1 to opposite sides of the pieced square created in Step 2. Repeat to make 4 of these rows.

4. Sew a 4½" red tonal square to the row pieced in Step 3. This completes the corner triangle. Repeat to make a total of 4 corner triangles.

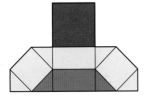

Sashing

1. Sew one 2½" x 14½" red floral sashing strip to the top and bottom of each basket block (Block A).
2. Sew one 2½" red tonal keystone square to each end of a remaining 2½" x 14½" red floral sashing strip. Repeat to make 2 short sashing strips.
3. Sew 3—2½" x 14½" red floral sashing strips and 4—2½" red tonal keystone squares together to make a long sashing strip. Repeat to make a second long sashing strip.

Quilt center

1. Referring to the quilt center assembly diagram below, arrange 4 basket blocks (Block A), one Block B, 4 setting triangles, 4 corner triangles, and sashing strips. Sew together in diagonal rows.

2. Referring to the quilt center assembly diagram, sew diagonal rows together.

Quilt Center Assembly Diagram

Home for the Holidays

3. Referring to the diagram below, trim the quilt center leaving a ¼" seam allowance to create tidy triangle points in the corners and outer sashing keystones. The quilt center should measure 45¾" x 45¾".

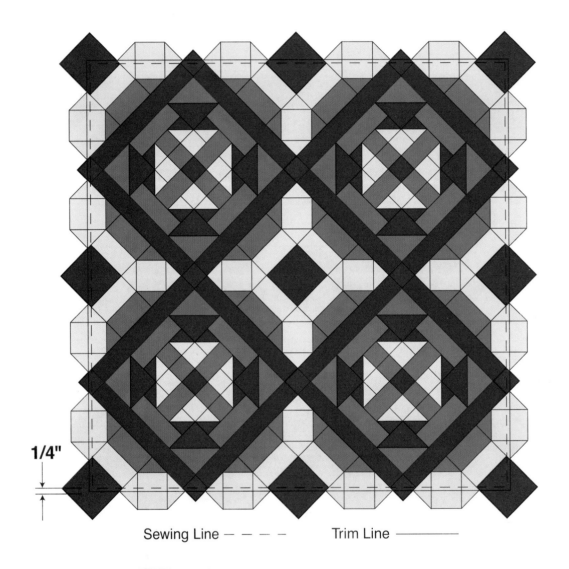

1/4"

Sewing Line — — — —   Trim Line ———

Backing Tip

Quilt backings are usually seamed in the middle, which can cause premature wear. That's because quilts are frequently folded in half, placing increased pressure on that seam. To prevent this dilemma, divide your backing fabric in half lengthwise. Then cut across and divide one piece of backing into two narrow vertical sections. Sew a narrow vertical section to each side of the larger piece of backing fabric. And don't forget to remove all selvages from the backing pieces.

Inner border

1. Referring to the assembly diagram below, sew a 2½" x 45¾" red tonal strip to the top and bottom of the quilt center.
2. Referring to the assembly diagram, sew a 2½" x 49¾" red tonal strip to both sides of the quilt center.

Outer border

1. Referring to the quilt assembly diagram, sew one 5¾" x 49¾" red large floral strip to the top and bottom of the quilt center.
2. Referring to the quilt assembly diagram, sew one 5¾" x 60¼" red large floral strip to both sides of the quilt center.

Quilt, bind, and enjoy.

Assembly Diagram

Quilts from One Block Design

As the popularity of whole cloth and medallion quilts waned in the second quarter of the 19th century, quilters began experimenting with designs of repeating blocks. Sometimes the blocks were placed directly next to each other. In other cases, they were separated by an alternate square or sashing. For our challenge, we opted to combine a single pieced block design with alternating squares—the perfect places to showcase our favorite quilting motifs and fabrics. This approach also keeps the focus on the pieced block.

Karen's quilt, Farmer's Daughter, features a simple pieced block in a variety of colors with alternating dark brown squares—an unusual choice for setting squares. Typically, a large-scale print would have been used for those areas, and that's the approach that Erin's quilt took. Southern Belle spotlights a lovely rose-themed fabric in the alternating squares. Combined with a pieced block featuring a square-in-a-square design within a nine-patch format, it makes a quick and easy bed quilt.

Farmer's Daughter

Designed by Karen Witt • Finished quilt size: 61¼" x 78¾" • Finished block size: 8¾"

Alternating plain squares of fabric with pieced blocks is a great way to create a simple yet striking quilt while reducing your fabric stash. Each of these Farmer's Daughter blocks was a joy to piece. For each block, I selected a light, medium, and dark fabric. Notice that the contrast between the fabric values varies from block to block, making this late 1800s-inspired quilt much more interesting than if they were all the same. I wanted to keep the focus on the pieced blocks, so I selected an alternating square in a small dark brown print that visually recedes.

FABRIC REQUIREMENTS

Farmer's Daughter blocks:

- ⅔ yard assorted tan/beige prints OR 5" square each of 32 tan/beige prints for 4 squares in 9-patch
- 1⅔ yard medium/dark prints OR 10" square each of 32 medium/dark prints for 5 squares in 9-patch and points of block
- 2 yards assorted light prints OR approximately 7" square each of 32 prints for block backgrounds

Dark brown setting squares and binding:

- 2¾ yards dark brown print

CUTTING INSTRUCTIONS

All measurements include ¼" seam allowances.

For pieced Farmer's Daughter blocks, cut:

- 128—2¼" squares from assorted tan/beige prints.
- 160—2¼" squares from assorted medium/dark prints.
- 256—2¼" squares from the same medium/dark prints listed above. (For each block, the "points" are the same fabrics as the 5 squares in the 9-patch unit.)
- 128—2¼" squares from light prints that coordinate with the medium/dark prints.
- 128—2¼" x 5¾" "B" rectangles from the same light prints listed above (These form part of the block background, which uses the same fabric as the four corner background squares).

For setting squares, cut:

- 31—9¼" squares from dark brown print.

For binding, cut:

- 290" x 2¼" strips from dark brown print. Then piece strips together end to end.

Farmer's Daughter

SEWING INSTRUCTIONS

Use a ¼" seam allowance and sew all pieces right sides together. Press seams toward the darker fabric.

Farmer's Daughter block

1. Sew together 5—2¼" medium/dark print squares and 4—2¼" light print squares to make a 5¾" nine-patch block.

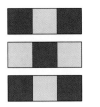

2. Place a 2¼" medium/dark print square on each end of a 2¼" x 5¾" tan/beige print rectangle. Referring to the diagram below, draw a diagonal line across the two squares. Repeat for a total of 4 units per block.

3. Sew on the diagonal line of each 2¼" medium/dark print square. Press. Then trim a ¼" from the sewn line. Repeat to make 4 of these units per block.

4. Referring to the top and bottom rows of the diagram below, sew a 2¼" tan/beige print square to opposite sides of the unit created in Step 3. Repeat to make a total of 2 of these rows per block.

5. Referring to the previous diagram, sew two of the units created in Step 3 to opposite sides of a nine-patch unit created in Step 1.

6. Sew together the two rows created in Step 4 and one row created in Step 5.

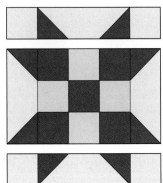 

7. Repeat Steps 1-6 to make a total of 32 blocks.

Batting

Quilts made in the 1800s tend to have thin battings. A quilter of that time period would have used whatever fiber she had on hand for batting—cotton, wool, straw, even newspaper! Commercial glazed batting was available for home use by 1848. However, rural quilters could make their own batting by carding cotton or wool from their farm crops or animals. Laying the tufts of carded fiber side by side onto the wrong side of the backing fabric, they created the thin, sometimes lumpy batting seen in many antique quilts. If closely quilted, the fibers would hold together relatively well. To recreate this antique look today, select batting made from 100% cotton or wool. Silk batting works great for hand quilting and gives your quilts a soft, antique appearance.

Farmer's Daughter

FINISHING THE QUILT

❖ Referring to the assembly diagram on page 35, lay out the pieced Farmer's Daughter blocks and alternating dark brown setting squares in 9 rows. Sew each row. Then sew the rows together.

QUILTING THE QUILT

❖ With its multiple patches and fabrics, the pieced blocks of Farmer's Daughter do not lend themselves to ornate quilting designs. Baptist Fan, a series of concentric circular motifs, and Hanging Diamonds, a series of parallel vertical rows stitched over with a series of diagonal parallel rows that create a diagonal design, are excellent choices for a late-1800s reproduction quilt like Farmer's Daughter.

❖ Quilters of this era often used white thread and widely-spaced diagonal lines when machine quilting. At the time, a sewing machine was a status symbol, and those who were able to afford one wanted to show off their stitching with bold quilting designs. If hand quilting this project, diagonal parallel lines would be an excellent choice. Primitive or utility stitches, using #12 perle cotton and a large embroidery needle to make approximately 4-6 stitches per inch, would also be period-appropriate.

BINDING THE QUILT

❖ Today most quilters prefer double-fold binding because of its durability and tidy mitered corners. In contrast, the binding on antique quilts is often sloppy and poorly applied. Perhaps those quilters of the past realized that the binding would inevitably need repair, and therefore, did not spend much time making it. To combine the look of antique bindings with 21st-century durability standards, use 2¼" strips cut along the straight grain of the fabric. Piece as necessary with a diagonal seam and butt the ends at the corners instead of mitering them.

Assembly Diagram

Southern Belle

Designed by Erin Witt • Finished quilt size: 73" x 97" • Finished block size: 12"

Having lived in Kentucky most of my life, I have an appreciation for Southern hospitality. The many wonderful beds-and-breakfasts that dot this part of the country inspired me to make this bed-sized quilt, which I envisioned would be right at home in one of their guest rooms. This luscious quilt allowed me to bring the romance and grace of a Southern bed-and-breakfast to the guest room of my own home. The feature fabric is a lovely large-scale rose-themed print. I used only three other coordinating fabrics, giving the overall design a simple, clean look. For the quilting design, I chose a large rose motif in the center of each alternating floral square block to echo the beauty of the focal fabric.

FABRIC REQUIREMENTS

Pieced blocks, blue inner and outer borders, floral border, and binding:

- 1¼ yards cream dot
- 2¼ yards blue floral
  (this is also used for the binding)
- 2¾ yards yellow floral

Setting squares:

- 2¼ yards pink large floral or more if fussy cutting your fabric

---

Two Quilts in One

I made this quilt reversible by backing it with a fabric in the same blue hue of the large floral print, matching the design elements at the seam for a smooth finish. For the cost of an extra yard of backing fabric, I was able to double the design possibilities of my quilt. With the simple flip of a quilt, I can totally change the décor of my room!

CUTTING INSTRUCTIONS

Measurements include a ¼" seam allowance.

For yellow floral border, cut:
These strips must be cut **before** the pieced blocks.
- 2—4½" x 62½" length of fabric strips from yellow floral for top and bottom border.
- 2—4½" x 95" length of fabric strips from yellow floral for side borders.

For the pieced blocks, cut:
- 180—2⅞" squares from cream dot. Then cut those squares in half once diagonally to create 360 triangles.
- 90—3⅜" squares from blue floral.
- 72—4½" squares from yellow floral.

For the setting squares, cut:
- 17—12½" squares from pink large floral. If fussy cutting, be sure to center the large floral motif on the square.

For inner and outer blue border, cut:
- 2—1½" x 84½" strips for the inner side borders.
- 2—1½" x 62½" strips for the inner top and bottom border.
- 2—1½" x 95" strips for the outer side borders.
- 2—1½" x 73" strips for the outer top and bottom border.

For binding, cut:
- 9—2½" x 42" strips from blue floral. Then piece strips together end to end.

SEWING INSTRUCTIONS

Use a ¼" seam allowance and sew all pieces with right sides together. Press seams toward the darker fabric.

Pieced block

1. Sew a cream dot triangle to each side of a 3⅜" blue floral square to create a square-in-a-square unit. Trim the unit to measure 4½" square, making sure the triangle points overlap each other a ¼" at the ends. Repeat to make a total of five units per block.

2. Noting the orientation of the yellow floral fabric in the photo on page 37, stitch the square-in-a-square units from Step 1 alternately with 4—4½" yellow floral squares to make one 12½" x 12½" block.

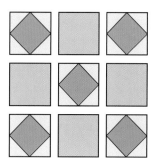

3. Repeat Steps 1 and 2 to make a total of 18 pieced blocks.

Finishing the quilt

1. Referring to the diagrams below and noting the orientation of blocks, sew the pieced blocks and pink large floral squares alternately together into seven horizontal rows of five blocks each. Press row seams in opposite directions.

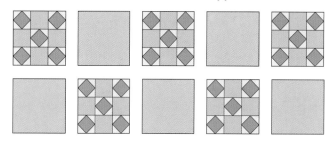

2. Referring to the assembly diagram on page 41, sew all the rows together to complete the quilt center. It should measure 60½" x 84½".

Southern Belle

Inner border

+ Referring to the assembly diagram on page 41, sew the 2—1½" x 84½" blue floral strips to the sides of the quilt center. Then sew the 2—1½" x 62½" blue floral strips to the top and bottom of the quilt center.

Middle border

+ Referring to the assembly diagram on page 41, sew the 2—4½" x 62½" yellow floral strips to the top and bottom of the quilt. Then sew the 2—4½" x 95" yellow floral strips to the sides of the quilt.

Outer border

+ Referring to the assembly diagram on page 41, sew the 2—1½" x 95" blue floral strips to the sides of the quilt. Then sew the 2—1½" x 73" blue floral strips to the top and bottom of the quilt.

Quilt, bind, and enjoy.

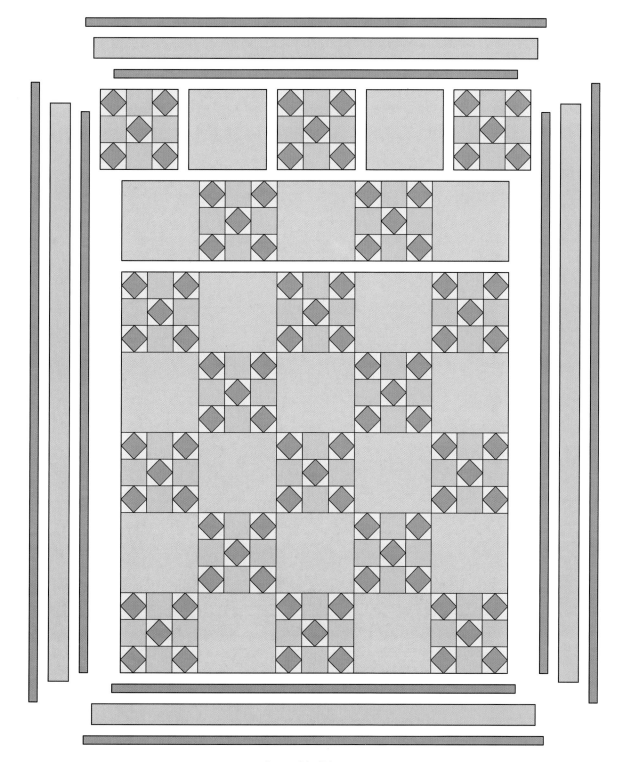

Assembly Diagram

Quick Quilts with a Twist

How many of us would quilt if we had to cut everything with scissors and stitch it all by hand? Inventive quilters have given us rotary cutters, sewing machines, fusible products, and notions that our predecessors wouldn't have even dreamed of! Thanks to these handy helpers, we can create heirloom-quality quilts in a fraction of the time.

Karen used fusible interfacing and machine appliqué to create the graphic stair-step border pattern in her Barrington Medallion quilt. A narrow machine buttonhole stitch quickly recreates the look of Broderie Perse, an 18th-century style of appliqué in which printed motifs are cut from expensive large-scale floral fabrics and appliquéd to a less expensive background fabric.

Erin's quilt, College Bound, is the perfect quilt-in-a-day project. It has only six large 24" blocks. Now that's quick! Because it is comprised of only squares and rectangles, you can cut out the quilt using a fast strip-set method. Large cornerstones dress up the border—a fuss-free solution for adding visual interest.

Barrington Medallion

Designed by Karen Witt · Finished quilt size: 53" x 53"

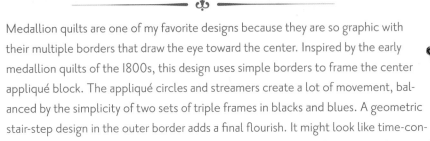

Medallion quilts are one of my favorite designs because they are so graphic with their multiple borders that draw the eye toward the center. Inspired by the early medallion quilts of the 1800s, this design uses simple borders to frame the center appliqué block. The appliqué circles and streamers create a lot of movement, balanced by the simplicity of two sets of triple frames in blacks and blues. A geometric stair-step design in the outer border adds a final flourish. It might look like time-consuming piecework, but the quilt's historically-recreated border design is machine appliquéd, greatly simplifying the process.

FABRIC REQUIREMENTS

Center appliqué block background and outer border:
- 1⅓ yards beige print

Center appliqué and squares in the square-in-a-square border:
- Fat quarter blue print
- Fat quarter gold print
- Fat quarter green print
- 3 fat quarters red prints

Large-scale black fabric yardage listed below under sixth heading

First, third, fifth, and seventh borders:
- ⅞ yard small dark print

Second and sixth borders:
- ½ yard medium blue print

Square-in-a-square border:
- ½ yard off-white print

Colored square yardage listed above under second heading

Outer border and binding:
- 1½ yards large-scale black print

Beige print yardage listed above under the first heading
- 2 yards lightweight fusible interfacing

CUTTING INSTRUCTIONS

Measurements include a ¼" seam allowance unless otherwise noted.

For center appliqué block, cut:
- 1—19" square from beige print for appliqué background.
- Templates on page 56 from assorted medium prints (Refer to photo on page 45 for color cues). Templates do **not** include a ¼" seam allowance. I used a raw-edge machine appliqué method.

For first border, cut:
- 2—1½" x 18½" strips from small dark print.
- 2—1½" x 20½" strips from small dark print.

For second border, cut:
- 2—1½" x 20½" strips from medium blue print.
- 2—1½" x 22½" strips from medium blue print.

For third border, cut:
- 2—1½" x 22½" strips from small dark print.
- 2—1½" x 24½" strips from small dark print.

For fourth border (square-in-a-square border), cut:
- 12—5¼" squares from off-white fabric. Then cut each square in half twice diagonally to make a total of 48 "B" triangles.
- 6—3" squares from off-white print. Then cut each square in half once diagonally to make 12 "A" triangles.
- 28—3⅜" squares from assorted medium prints for "C" squares.

For fifth border, cut:
- 2—2" x 32½" strips from small dark print.
- 2—2" x 35½" strips from small dark print.

Barrington Medallion

For sixth border, cut:

✦ 2—2" x 35½" strips from medium blue print.

✦ 2—2" x 38½" strips from medium blue print.

For seventh border, cut:

✦ 2—2" x 38½" strips from small dark print.

✦ 2—2" x 41½" strips from small dark print.

For eighth (outer border), cut:

✦ 4—4½" x 45" length of fabric strips from large-scale black print for the stair-step design. Before you cut these strips, it is a good idea to measure your quilt's width and length. It should be 41½" x 41½". If your measurements differ, adjust the border lengths accordingly.

✦ 4—7" x 7" squares from large-scale black print for the corner stair-step design.

✦ 2—6 ½" x 41½" strips from beige print.

✦ 2—6½" x 51½" strips from beige print.

✦ 4—4½" x 45" strips from lightweight fusible interfacing for stair-step appliqué strips.

✦ 4—7" x 7" squares from lightweight fusible interfacing for corner stair-step appliqué sections.

For binding, cut:

✦ 6—2¼" strips the length of fabric from large-scale black print. Then piece strips together end to end.

SEWING INSTRUCTIONS

Center appliqué block

1. Fold a 19" beige print square into quarters, then press diagonally to each of the four corners (This will help you accurately position the appliqué pieces).

2. Referring to the diagram below, appliqué the pieces created from the templates on page 56 to the 19" beige print background square. Press and trim this center block to 18½" x 18½".

First border

1. Referring to the quilt assembly diagram on page 48, sew one 1½" x 18½" small dark print strip to the top and bottom of the center appliqué block.

2. Referring to the quilt assembly diagram on page 48, sew one 1½" x 20½" small dark print strip to both sides of the center appliqué block. Press. The quilt top should now measure 20½" x 20½".

Second border

1. Referring to the quilt assembly diagram on page 48, sew one 1½" x 20½" medium blue print strip to the top and bottom of the quilt top.

2. Referring to the quilt assembly diagram on page 48, sew one 1½" x 22½" medium blue print strip to both sides of the quilt top. Press. The quilt top should now measure 22½" x 22½".

Third border

1. Referring to the quilt assembly diagram on page 48, sew one 1½" x 22½" small dark print strip to the top and bottom of the quilt top.

2. Referring to the quilt assembly diagram on page 48, sew one 1½" x 24½" small dark print strip to both sides of the quilt top. Press. The quilt top should now measure 24½" x 24½".

Fourth border (square-in-a-square border)

1. Referring to the diagram below, lay out "C" squares, "B" setting triangles, and "A" corner triangles for the top and bottom border strips. Then sew the segments together to create two strips. Press and trim each strip to 4½" x 24½".

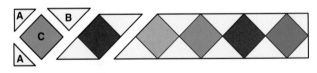

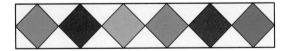

2. Referring to the quilt assembly diagram on page 48, sew the border strips created in Step 1 to the top and bottom of the quilt top.

3. Referring to the diagram below, lay out "C" squares, "B" setting triangles, and "A" corner triangles for the side border strips. Then sew the segments together to create two strips. Press and trim each strip to 4½" x 32½".

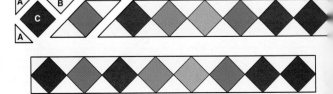

Barrington Medallion

4. Referring to the quilt assembly diagram below, sew the border strips created in Step 3 to each side of the quilt top. The quilt top should now measure 32½" x 32½".

Fifth border

1. Referring to the quilt assembly diagram, sew one 2" x 32½" small dark print strip to the top and bottom of the quilt top.
2. Referring to the quilt assembly diagram, sew one 2" x 35½" small dark print strip to both sides of the quilt top. Press. The quilt top should now measure 35½" x 35½".

Assembly Diagram

Sixth border

1. Referring to the quilt assembly diagram on page 48, sew one 2" x 35½" medium blue print strip to the top and bottom of the quilt top.
2. Referring to the quilt assembly diagram on page 48, sew one 2" x 38½" medium blue print strip to both sides of the quilt top. Press. The quilt top should now measure 38½" x 38½".

Seventh border

1. Referring to the quilt assembly diagram on page 48, sew one 2" x 38½" small dark print strip to the top and bottom of the quilt top.
2. Referring to the quilt assembly diagram on page 48, sew one 2" x 41½" small dark print strip to both sides of the quilt top. Press. The quilt top should now measure 41½" x 41½".

Eighth border

1. Referring to the quilt assembly diagram on page 48, sew one 5½" x 41½" beige print strip to the top and bottom of the quilt top.
2. Referring to the quilt assembly diagram on page 48, sew one 5½" x 51½" beige print strip to both sides of the quilt top. Press. The quilt top should now measure 51½" x 51½".

Barrington Medallion

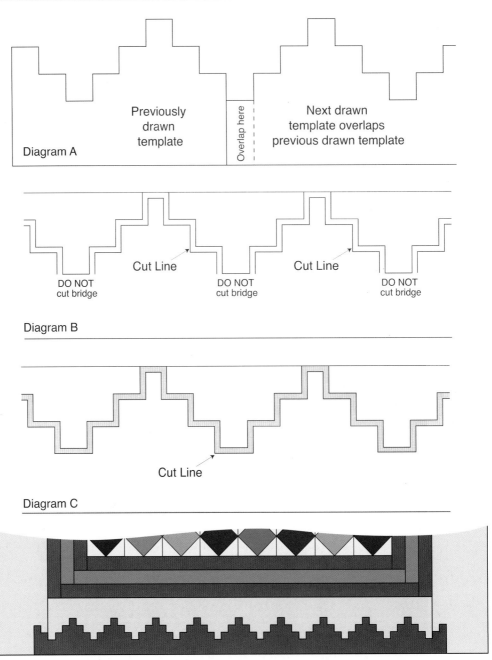

Diagram A

Previously drawn template

Overlap here

Next drawn template overlaps previous drawn template

Cut Line   Cut Line

DO NOT cut bridge   DO NOT cut bridge   DO NOT cut bridge

Diagram B

Cut Line

Diagram C

Diagram D

Eighth border appliqué

1. Using the stair-step templates on pages 54-55, trace around the templates on the paper side of the 4—4½" x 45" fusible interfacing strips, being careful to overlap the lowest stair-step on top of the previous template's stair-step so that all "steps" are the same size. Templates do **not** include a ¼" seam allowance since I used a raw-edge applique method. If doing needleturn applique, you will need to add a ¼" seam allowance. Referring to diagram A on this page, begin with the second to highest stair-step and create 4 strips like the one shown in diagram D on this page.

2. To prevent stiffness along the finished edge of the quilt, trim the fusible interfacing approximately ¼" inside the pencil line on the stair-step side **only** as shown in diagram B on this page. To avoid working with awkward long, thin pieces of fusible interfacing, I don't trim along the entire stair-step edge. Instead, I leave "bridges" of interfacing about every 3–4 inches that connect the top edge of the interfacing to the portion that you will discard later. It isn't necessary to leave bridges in the 4 corner stair-step sections since they are smaller pieces. Simply cut out a line of interfacing a ¼" inside the pencil line for those 4 pieces.

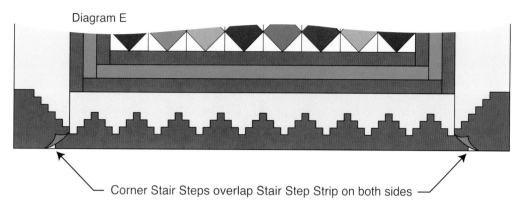

Diagram E

Corner Stair Steps overlap Stair Step Strip on both sides

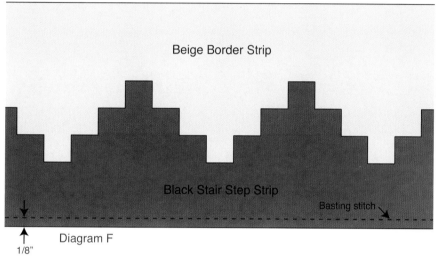

Beige Border Strip

Black Stair Step Strip

Basting stitch

1/8"

Diagram F

3. Align the 4—4½" x 45" fusible interfacing strips along the bottom edge of the 4—4½" x 45" large-scale black print stair-step border strips.

4. Align the 4—7" x 7" fusible interfacing squares with the 4—7" x 7" large-scale black print border corner stair-step sections.

5. Carefully fuse only the top edges of the 4—4½" x 45" large-scale black print stair-step strips to the 4—4½" x 45" fusible interfacing strips by lightly touching the iron to these areas. Do the same for the 4 corner stair-step sections.

6. Once the top edge of the fusible interfacing has been "tacked" or lightly ironed to the large-scale black print strips, carefully cut away the larger area of interfacing as shown in diagram C on page 50 and press them firmly to the large-scale black print strips.

7. Following the pencil line you marked earlier on the fusible interfacing, cut out the 4—4½" x 45" large-scale black print stair-step border strips and the 4—7" x 7" large-scale black print corner stair-step sections along the stair-step edge. The stair-step strips will now be 4" x 45" (4" being the height of the highest step of the stair-step pattern).

8. Remove the paper from the fusible interfacing. Referring to diagram D on page 50, center one large-scale black print stair-step border strip on each side of the beige print background borders.

9. Referring to diagram E on this page, place large-scale black print corner stair-step sections overlapping the 4" x 45" large-scale black print stair-step border strips. Trim the 4—4" x 45" large-scale black print stair-step border strips so that the 4 large-scale black print corner stair-step sections overlap them by a ½". It is best to work with one side of the quilt at a time rather than trying to position all 4 stair-step strips and 4 corner stair-step sections at once. This way, you can make adjustments as needed.

10. Referring to diagram F on this page, baste the bottom edge of the 4" x 45" large-scale black print stair-step strip and 2 large-scale black print corner stair-step sections in place ⅛" from the edge to secure them while stitching. Because they will be concealed beneath the binding, which is stitched ¼" away from the edge, the basting stitches won't need to be removed, unless you wish—another time-savvy tip! Continue basting the remaining stair-step strips and corner border sections in place—one side at a time.

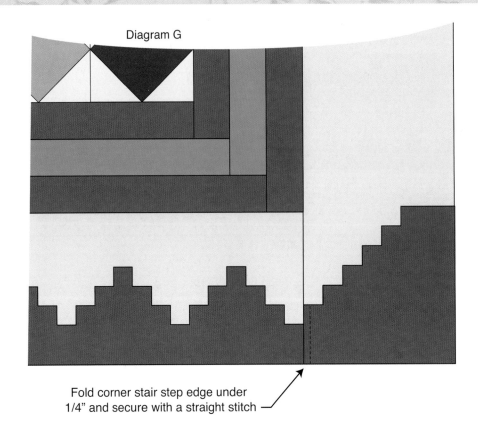

Diagram G

Fold corner stair step edge under
1/4" and secure with a straight stitch —

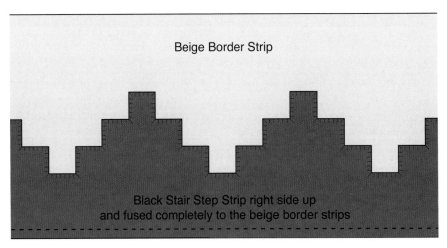

Beige Border Strip

Black Stair Step Strip right side up
and fused completely to the beige border strips

Diagram H

11. Turn the raw edges of the 4 large-scale black print corner stair-step border sections under ¼" where they overlap the 4—4" x 45" large-scale black print stair-step border strips. Referring to diagram G on this page, sew a straight stitch ⅛" from their edge to secure them.

12. To secure the appliqué, sew a machine buttonhole stitch along the entire stair-step edge as shown in diagram H on this page. I like to miter the stitching at the inside and outside corners of the stair-steps.

19th-Century Appliqué Quilt Border Designs

The outer appliquéd border featured in Barrington Medallion is often called the Tidewater Stair Step because it is most commonly seen in early quilts of the Virginia and Maryland coastal regions. Other popular appliqué border designs of the 1800s included Saw Tooth, which resembles a shallow Flying Geese unit; Scallop, which resembles a fluted piecrust; and Dog Tooth, a jagged-edge pattern rarely seen after 1850. To replicate the latter motif, contemporary quilters often use a border of half-square triangles in two fabrics.

Susan's Simple Appliqué Border Template

An easy alternative to making your own stair-step border templates is the handy Susan's Simple Appliqué Border™—an acrylic ruler that makes speedy work of creating a stair-step pattern. It is available from Reproduction Quilts. To order, go to www.reproductionquilts.com or call 859/333-6232.

Recreating Broderie Perse

To replicate the look of antique Broderie Perse, use thread that matches the appliqué shapes. Set your sewing machine with a narrow, short buttonhole stitch. Be sure to secure your threads by pulling them through to the back of the quilt and tying them. Some newer machines have a knotting button that makes faster work of securing the threads.

QUILTING THE QUILT

❖ Antique medallion quilts are usually stitched with geometric patterns—diagonal lines, chevron lines, cross hatching, or hanging diagonals. Other popular designs include concentric circles, clamshells, loops, and feathers. To quilt parallel diagonal lines or cross hatching, start at one corner of the quilt and mark a diagonal line to the opposite corner. Quilt about 1–2" apart across the quilt. Masking tape or painter's tape works well for marking the design. To avoid leaving a sticky residue, be sure to remove it at the end of each quilting session.

BINDING THE QUILT

❖ 19th-century quilts were often finished by turning the front or back to the other side in a narrow rolled hemmed edge. If you want to achieve that same period look in your version of Barrington Medallion, bind using the 2¼" wide strips. Or if you prefer, use 1½" straight-grain binding and machine stitch it to the front of quilt. Then turn the fabric to the back of the quilt and whipstitch the edge down to make a narrow, soft single-fold binding. For an authentic-looking 1800s-style quilt, make the corners square or butted, not mitered.

Batting

A thin cotton or wool batting would be the most appropriate choice for a replica of a circa 1830 medallion quilt. There are also silk battings currently available that are great for hand quilting and give a soft, antique appearance.

Barrington Medallion

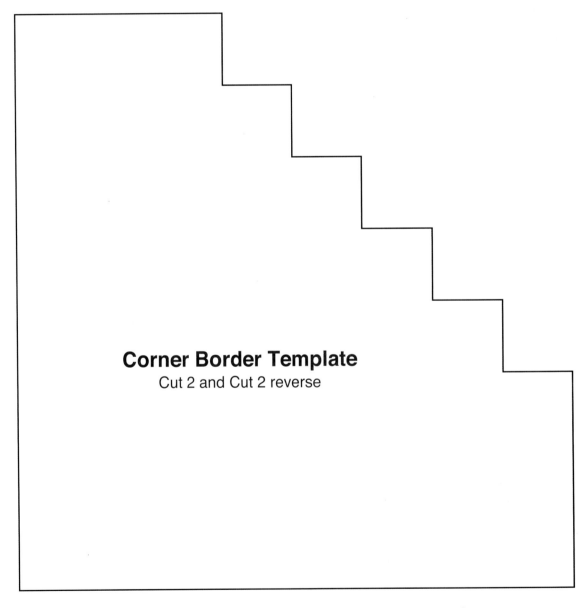

Corner Border Template
Cut 2 and Cut 2 reverse

Add ¼" seam allowance for needleturn appliqué.

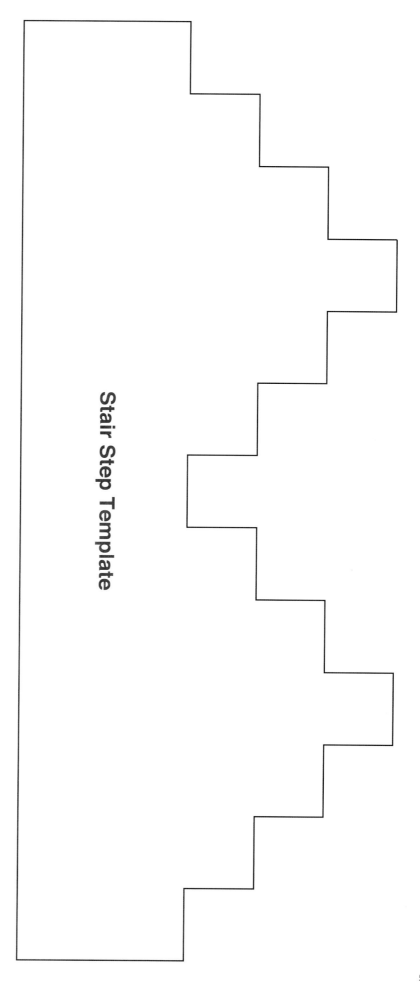

Stair Step Template

Add 1/4" seam allowance for needleturn appliqué.

Barrington Medallion

Add ¼" seam allowance for needleturn appliqué.

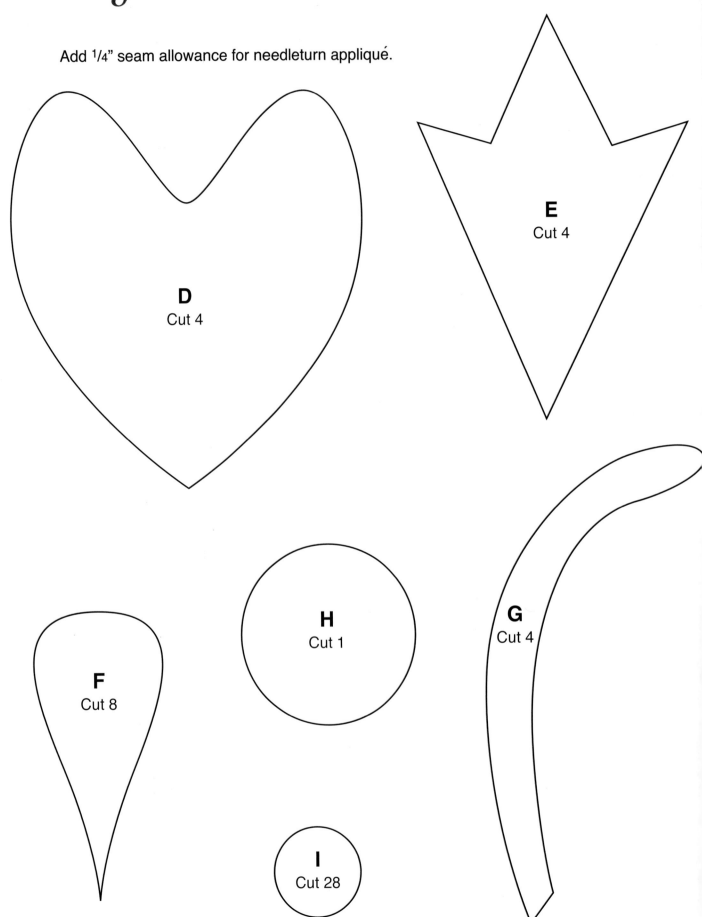

D
Cut 4

E
Cut 4

F
Cut 8

H
Cut 1

G
Cut 4

I
Cut 28

College Bound

Designed by Erin Witt • Finished quilt size: 61" x 85" • Finished block size: 24"

This twin-size quilt is a wonderful project for a beginning quilter or for an experienced quilter in a rush! It makes a fun gift for a college student, too. Its bright colors and simple design are sure to brighten up even the dullest of dorm rooms, wrapping the lucky recipient in love and support on those long nights studying far away from the comforts of home.

FABRIC REQUIREMENTS

Pieced blocks, border cornerstones, and binding:

- 1¾ yards purple print
- 1⅛ yards purple floral
- 1 yard pink print
- 1 yard pink floral

Border:

- 2⅛ yards pink stripe

CUTTING INSTRUCTIONS

Measurements include a ¼" seam allowance.

For the pieced blocks, cut:

- 6—9" "A" squares.
- 12—6⅞" squares. Then cut squares in half once diagonally to make 24 "B" triangles.
- 24—6⅞" squares. Then cut squares in half once diagonally to make 48 "B" triangles.
- 9—3½" x 42" strips from pink print.
- 9—3½" x 42" strips from pink floral.

For border, cut:

- 2—7" x 72½" strips from pink stripe for side borders.
- 2—7" x 48½" strips from pink stripe for top and bottom borders.
- 4—7" squares from purple print for cornerstones.

For binding, cut:

- 8—2¼" strips the width of fabric from purple print. Then piece strips together end to end.

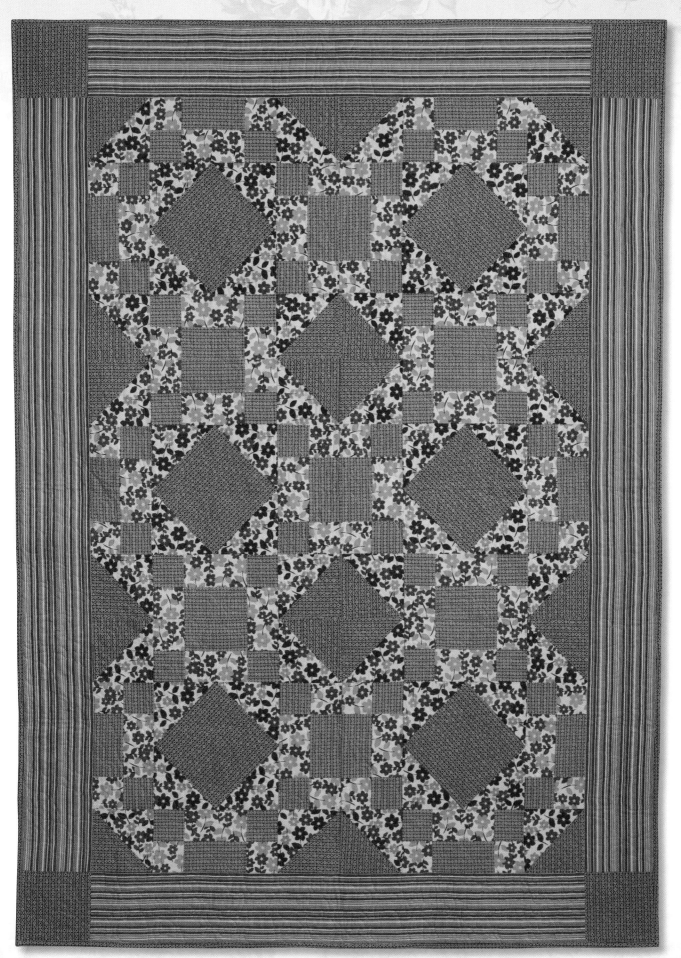

SEWING INSTRUCTIONS
Use a ¼" seam allowance and sew pieces right sides together. Press seams toward darker fabric.

Pieced blocks
1. Sew 4 purple floral "B" triangles to all sides of one purple
   print "A" square to create a 12½" square-in-a-square unit.
   Repeat to make a total of 6 units.

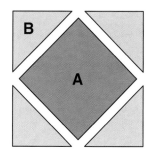
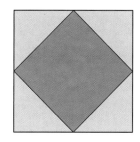

2. Sew 1 purple print "B" triangle to 1 purple floral "B" triangle to make a half-square triangle unit. Repeat to make
   a total of 24 of these units.

3. Sew 1—3½" x 42" pink print strip to 1—3½" x 42" pink
   floral strip. Repeat to make a total of 9 strip sets. From
   these strip sets, cut 48—3½" x 6½" "C" units and
   24—6½" x 6½" "D" units.

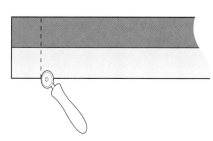

4. Sew one "C" unit to opposite sides of a "D" unit. Repeat to
   make a total of 24 of these rows.

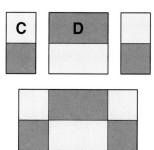

5. Sew one side unit created in Step 4 to opposite sides of a
   12½" square-in-a-square unit created in Step 1. Repeat to
   make a total of 6 of these rows for the center row of each
   of the 6 blocks.

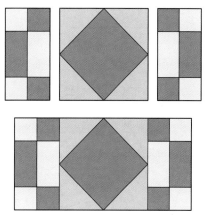

6. Referring to the top and bottom rows in the diagram
   below, sew one half-square triangle unit created in Step 2
   to each side of the unit created in Step 4. Repeat to make
   12 rows for the top and bottom rows of each block.

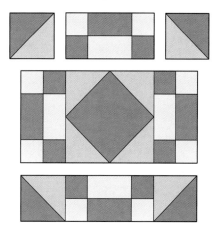

7. Referring to the following diagram, sew two rows created
   in Step 6 to the top and bottom of the center row created
   in Step 5. This completes the block. Repeat to make a
   total of 6 blocks.

College Bound

FINISHING THE QUILT

1. Referring to the assembly diagram below, lay out all the pieced blocks and sew them together in rows. Then sew the rows together.
2. Referring to the assembly diagram, sew 2—7" x 72½" pink stripe border strips to both sides of the quilt center.
3. Referring to the assembly diagram, sew one 7" purple print square to each end of the 2—7" x 48½" top and bottom border strips.
4. Referring to the assembly diagram, sew the 2—7" x 61½" pink stripe border strips to the top and bottom of the quilt center.
5. Quilt, bind, and enjoy.

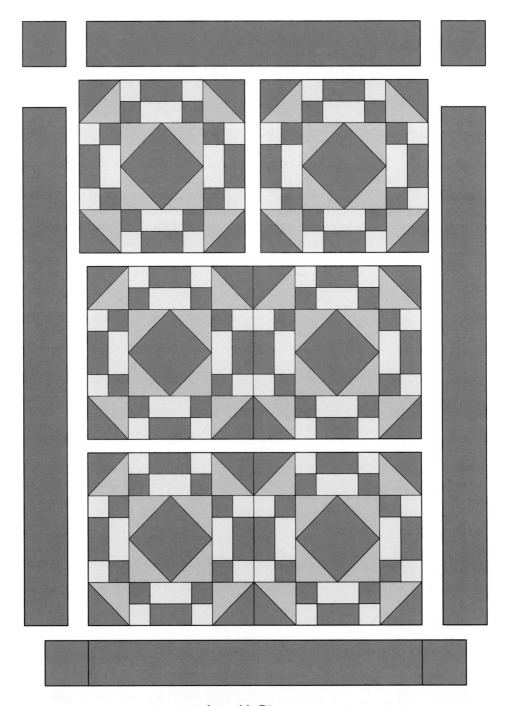

Assembly Diagram

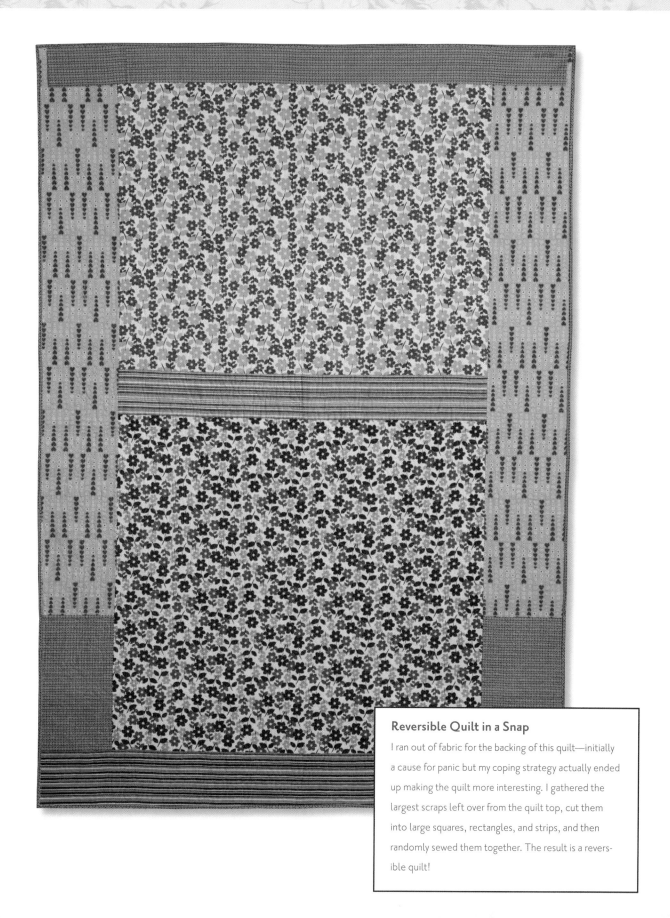

Reversible Quilt in a Snap

I ran out of fabric for the backing of this quilt—initially a cause for panic but my coping strategy actually ended up making the quilt more interesting. I gathered the largest scraps left over from the quilt top, cut them into large squares, rectangles, and strips, and then randomly sewed them together. The result is a reversible quilt!

Multi-Sided Designs

Multi-sided designs make dramatic statements in both of our quilts, but we took different approaches to their styles and construction. Karen enjoys the process of hand piecing hexagons and was inspired to create a quilt that showcased them. Long before quilters fell in love with the 1930s Grandmother's Flower Garden pattern, their 18th-century predecessors were using hexagons to create mosaic or honeycomb quilts. Karen's quilt, Tillie's Mosaic, spotlights the beautiful toiles and chintzes of that era with fussy-cut fabrics interspersed among the pieced hexagons. Erin's quilt, Columbine Clusters, makes a dramatic statement with a simpler, easy-to-make multi-sided design. At first glance, it might look complicated, but it comes together easily with a large Snowball block and an alternating Variable Star block.

Tillie's Mosaic

Designed by Karen Witt · Finished quilt size: 65½" x 68¾"

❦

I once read an article that showed how to sew hexagons together by machine, but I was just not interested. I enjoy the process of hand piecing them. There is a saying in the quilting world—"Making a quilt is a process, not a product"—and I very much follow that philosophy. The Y seams that are so difficult to achieve by machine are much easier to accomplish when hand piecing. Inspired by the exquisite mosaic quilts of the 1820s, this quilt combines pieced hexagons and fussy-cut fabrics. It is a great project to work on when you're on the go. Simply cut out the hexagons ahead of time, organize them into rosette and flower units (see key below), pack your sewing kit, and you're ready to go!

FABRIC REQUIREMENTS

Hexagons and 4 large fussy-cut areas:

- 3 yards assorted medium/dark prints
- 2½ yards beige solid or light tonal for row of light-colored hexagons surrounding each rosette unit (Referred to as beige solid from here)

Outer border, large central fussy-cut area, some fussy-cut rosettes, and binding:

- 2 yards large floral print

CUTTING INSTRUCTIONS

Measurements include a ¼" seam allowance.

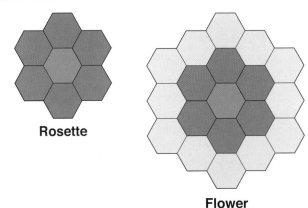

Rosette

Flower

For each rosette unit (you will need a total of 31 units), cut:

- 6 hexagon templates on page 73 from medium/dark print.
- 1 hexagon template on page 73 from a coordinating medium/dark print to the medium/dark print listed above.

For each partial top path (you will need a total of 5 units), cut:

- 3 hexagon templates on page 73 from medium/dark print.
- Beige solid hexagons needed are included on page 68, but you will need 5 of them for each partial bottom path. These will be joined by an additional single beige solid hexagon.

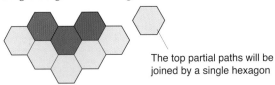

The top partial paths will be joined by a single hexagon

Top Partial Path

Tillie's Mosaic

For each partial bottom path (you will need a total of 5 units), cut:

- ⁜ 1 hexagon template on page 73 from medium/dark print.
- ⁜ Beige solid hexagons needed are included below, but you will need 5 of them for each partial bottom path.

Bottom Partial Path

For each partial side path (you will need a total of 8 units), cut:

- ⁜ 2 hexagon templates on page 73 from medium/dark print.
- ⁜ Beige solid hexagons needed are included below, but you will need 3 of them for each partial side path.

Side Partial Path

For each partial bottom corner path (you will need a total of 2 units), cut:

- ⁜ 1 hexagon template on page 73 from medium/dark print.
- ⁜ Beige solid hexagons needed are included below, but you will need 4 of them for each partial bottom corner path.

Right bottom corner (reverse for opposite left bottom corner)

Bottom Corner Partial Path

For each partial top corner path (you will need a total of 2 units), cut:

- ⁜ 3 hexagon templates on page 73 from medium/dark print.
- ⁜ Beige solid hexagons needed are included below, but you will need 4 of them for each partial top corner path.

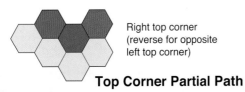

Right top corner (reverse for opposite left top corner)

Top Corner Partial Path

For each fussy-cut rosette, cut:

- ⁜ 9 fussy-cut hexagon templates on page 73 from assorted medium/dark prints.

For flower units and partial path units, cut:

- ⁜ 567 hexagons from beige solid (These will then be sewn to the rosette unit).

For multicolor hexagon path that connects the rosette units, cut:

- ⁜ 299 hexagon templates on page 73 from assorted medium/dark prints.

For 5 large fabric areas, cut:
- 5—12" squares from a large-scale fabric such as a floral, chintz, or toile.

For border, cut:
You may want to wait until the hexagon quilt center is completed before cutting border strips. There are many seam allowances and even slight variations multiplied by the large number of seams may cause the dimensions to vary.

- 2—4½" x 57¼" length of fabric strips from large floral print for top and bottom borders.
- 2—4½" x 68¾" length of fabric strips from large floral print for side borders.

For binding, cut:
- 290" x 2¼" length of fabric strips from large floral print.

Tillie's Mosaic

SEWING INSTRUCTIONS

Use a ¼" seam allowance and sew pieces right sides together. Press seams toward darker fabric.

1. Sew 6 medium/dark print hexagons and one central coordinating medium/dark print hexagon together to create a rosette unit. Repeat to create a total of 31 pieced rosettes (You should also have the 9 fussy-cut rosettes you cut earlier).

2. Sew a row of 12 beige solid hexagons around 34 of the rosettes (27 pieced and 7 fussy-cut) to create a flower unit.

3. Sew 9 beige solid hexagons to the top, bottom, and side of remaining 6 rosettes (4 pieced and 2 fussy cut). Referring to the diagram below, sew them to the sides of the quilt center.

4. Referring to the diagrams on pages 66 and 68, piece together the partial top and bottom, side, and corner paths.

5. Referring to the quilt center assembly diagram below, piece the 7 rows together, connecting the flower units created in Step 2 with a "path" of assorted medium/dark print hexagons. Attach the necessary partial side, top and bottom, and corner paths to the quilt center. Leave openings for the 5 large areas where you will later place the 12" fussy-cut fabric squares.

6. To attach the 5—12" fussy-cut fabric squares, first fold back and finger press the seam allowances of the surrounding hexagons. Then place the 12" fabric squares underneath the quilt top and appliqué the hexagon folded edges on to the squares. Carefully trim excess fabric from the 12" square.

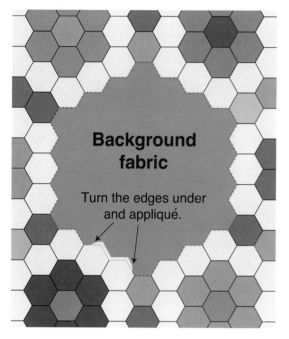

7. Referring to the diagram below, trim the quilt center, leaving a ¼" seam allowance.

1/4"→|←   Sew line – – – – –   Trim line ———————

8. Before cutting and attaching borders, measure your quilt center first and then cut them to size accordingly. Referring to the quilt assembly diagram on page 72, sew the 2—4½" x 57¼" large floral print strips to the top and bottom of the quilt center.

9. Before cutting and attaching borders, measure your quilt center first and then cut them to size accordingly. Referring to the quilt assembly diagram on page 72, sew the 2—4½" x 68¾" large floral print strips to opposite sides of the quilt center.

Templates Made Easy

You can speed up the process of making hexagonal templates with this handy rubber stamp developed by Kathleen Ackley. For best results, work on a flat surface. Ink the stamp with fabric-safe ink, then position it along the bottom edge of the fabric. Gently press. Continue working across the fabric in a row until you create the necessary number of templates. For ease, the rubber stamp is marked with a cutting and stitching line. Simply cut along the solid outside line and stitch the units together along the dotted lines. This stamp as well as fabric-safe ink are available from Reproduction Quilts. To order, log on to www.reproductionquilts.com or call 859-333-6232.

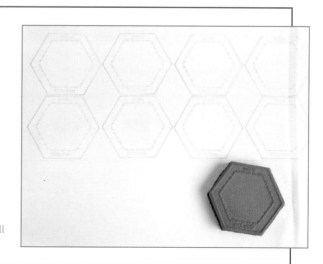

Tillie's Mosaic

Assembly Diagram

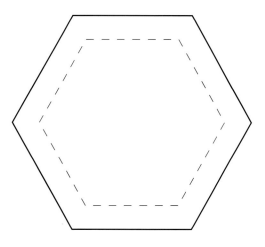

These templates include
a 1/4" seam allowance

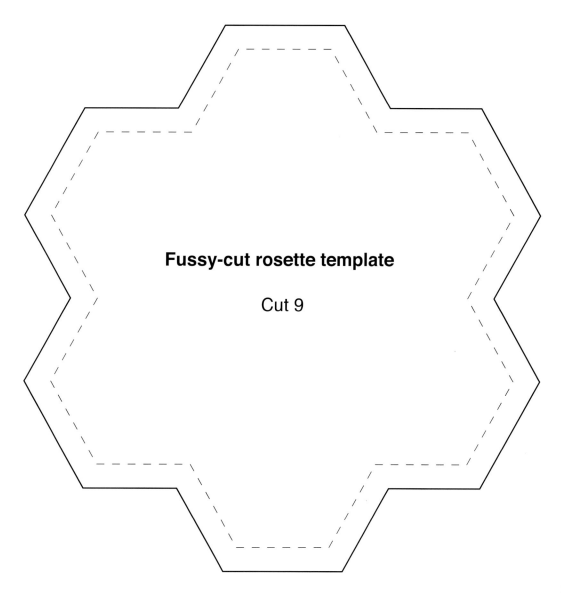

Fussy-cut rosette template

Cut 9

Dust Ruffle

A dust ruffle is a quick and decorative way to complement your Tillie's Mosaic quilt. If you tend to store items under your bed, it is also a great way to conceal the clutter. Traditionally, dust ruffles were made to fit between the mattress and box springs. Today's quicker techniques make construction faster and removal for laundering much easier. To create a dust ruffle, first measure the drop of your bed. This is the distance from the top of the box-spring to the floor. Add 2½" for hemming the bottom and a ½" for the gathering at the top. To find out how much fabric you will need, multiply this number by the number of panels you will need from the chart below. For example, a tall queen size bed with a 22" drop will require 22" + 2.5" + .5" for each panel. That's a total of 25". Multiply that figure by 10 panels for a queen size bed, and you need 250" of fabric, or the equivalent of 6.94 yards (round up to 7 yards).

INSTRUCTIONS

1. Sew the required number of panels together to make a dust ruffle for one side of the bed. Repeat for the other side.
2. Sew the required number of panels together to make the dust ruffle for the end of the bed.
3. Stitch a narrow hem along the outside vertical edges—the left and right sides of the dust ruffle.
4. Mark the bottom edge of the fabric for a 2½" hem. Hem this edge, turning ¼" of the fabric inside for a neat finish.
5. Use a serger or zig-zag stitch to overcast the top edge of the panels.
6. With your stitch length set to about 8 stitches per inch, gather the top of the panels by sewing two parallel stitching lines. Gather by pulling the bobbin threads (Their tension is generally looser than the top threads and will pull easier).
7. Ease the gathers to the size you need. For example, gather a dust ruffle section for the bottom of a queen size bed to 60". Stabilize the gathering stitches by stitching through them with a regular length stitch.
8. Sew or glue a long strip of Velcro to the back side of the top of the dust ruffle. Some modern mattresses are heavy enough to hold the dust ruffle in place without Velcro. If this is the case with your mattress, after Step 7, sew a strip of fabric 6½" by the length of the end of the mattress to the gathered dust ruffle. Fold the strip in half and hem to create a "waistband" for the dust ruffle. Push the band between the mattress and box-springs. If necessary, spiral upholstery pins will help secure the dust ruffle.
9. Attach the other side of the Velcro strip to the top of the box-spring by stitching, gluing, pining with spiral upholstery pins, or using a staple gun.
10. Fasten Velcro strips together for a beautiful dust ruffle without the hassle of moving the mattress.

Bed Size	Number of Panels to Cut for End	Number of Panels to Cut for Each Side	Total Panels to Cut
Crib (23" x 46")	1	2	5
Twin (39" x 75")	1.75	3.25	9
Double (54" x 75")	2.5	3.25	9
Queen (60" x 80")	2.75	3.5	10
King (76" x 80")	3.5	3.5	11
California King (72" x 84")	3	3.75	11

Hexagon Block in History

Godey's Lady's Book published the hexagon block—thought to be the first pieced quilt pattern published in America—in 1835. The article in the January issue that year proclaimed, "There is not patchwork that is prettier or more ingenious ... than the hexagon or six-sided honeycomb patchwork." The earliest hexagon quilts appear to have been sewn without any regard for color arrangement. However, it wasn't long before design-savvy quilters began experimenting with fussy cutting and creating color-coordinated kaleidoscope-type rosettes.

Roman Shade

Roman shades add a soft, casual look to your room while providing privacy. And when lowered, they showcase your selected fabric. They can be dressed up with trims and stripes, but their beauty lies in their simplicity. Here's how to create coordinating roman shades for your Tillie's Mosaic quilt.

INSTRUCTIONS

1. Measure the window. Add 4" to the width and 8½" to the length. Cut your fabric and lining fabric to size. If sewing sections of fabric together to make the shade, do this first.

2. Lay fabric right side down on a large flat surface. Fold and press 2" hems on long sides and base. Miter and slip-stitch corners. Hem sides and base by hand (or machine if you don't mind visible stitches).

3. Lay lining right side down. Fold and press a 2⅜" hem on long sides and base. Place lining on shade, wrong sides facing so that shade fabric shows slightly on long sides and base. Slipstitch lining to shade on hemmed sides.

4. Determine positions of dowel pockets, which will be placed horizontally across the shade, and mark them on the back of the shade with a disappearing ink pen. Pockets should be evenly spaced at intervals of 8-12" (depending on how wide you want the pleats to be). Begin measuring and marking intervals from the bottom and don't worry about the precise measurement of the top interval. To determine the position of the bottom pocket, divide the size of intervals by 2, and add 1. For example, if you're spacing dowels 12" apart, the bottom pocket should be 7" from the bottom of the shade and the top pocket should be at least 10" from the top.

5. Using lining fabric, sew cotton strips for dowel rods by cutting a strip of fabric 3½" by the width of the shade, minus 4". Fold fabric in half with wrong sides together and make a tube, using a ¼" seam. Turn the tube. Machine stitch a ¼" seam along the long sewn edge. Pin folded long edge of pocket along pen marks and machine stitch in place. Insert dowel (or hollow ½" PVC pipe) and slip-stitch the end closed.

6. Draw a line 6½" below the top of the shade. Wrap batten ends (strip of wood used at top of shade for support) in fabric swatches and staple. Roll and staple batten until edge covers marker line.

7. Stitch small plastic rings to the hemmed edges of dowel pockets, forming three columns, one up the center and the outside ones 2" from each long side. Attach cord lock (a fastener used to lock the shade in place by gathering the cords) to batten ¼" in from its edge on side where strings will fall. Attach a screw eye to batten at top of remaining ring rows.

8. In each row, starting at bottom of shade, tie the end of a length of cord to the lowest ring. Thread cord through rings in that row, through screw eyes at top, then through cord lock. Thread loose ends through cord condenser; knot below, trim two of the cords, and pull condenser down to cover knot. Cut remaining cord so that it hangs two thirds of the way down the shade. Thread through tassel and tie knot to secure. Then mount shade with appropriate hardware.

Columbine Clusters

Designed by Erin Witt • Finished quilt size: 90" x 108" • Finished block size: 12"

Creating a dramatic multi-sided design doesn't have to take a lot of time. I made quick work of it by simply cutting off the corners of a square to form a Snowball block, which alternates with an easy-to-make Variable Star block. To generate visual movement, I added half-square triangles to the star block corners. Inspired by the peaceful feeling of a meadow, the quilt's color palette works well for both feminine and masculine tastes, making it a great accent for the master bedroom.

FABRIC REQUIREMENTS

Snowball blocks and binding:
- 3 yards cream floral (also used for the binding)
- 3⅛ yards brown with blue floral print (also used in Variable Star blocks and first border)

Variable Star blocks:
- ½ yard blue with rust geometric print for star centers
- 1⅛ yards rust circular print for triangular star corners
- 1⅛ yards blue with rust floral print for star points

Brown with blue floral print for star backgrounds yardage is listed in previous heading

First border:
Brown with blue floral print yardage is listed in first heading

Second border:
- 1 yard blue zig-zag print

Third border:
- 2½ yards brown with blue geometric print

CUTTING INSTRUCTIONS
Measurements include a ¼" seam allowance.

For the Snowball blocks, cut:
- 17—12½" squares from cream floral.
- 68—3½" squares from brown with blue floral.

For the Variable Star blocks, cut:
- 22—4¾" squares from blue with rust geometric print for star centers.
- 88—3⅞" squares from rust circular print for triangular star corners. Then cut those 88 squares in half once diagonally to create 176 triangles.
- 88—3⅞" squares from blue with rust floral print for star points. Then cut those squares in half once diagonally to create 176 triangles.
- 22—7¼" squares from brown with blue floral for star background. Then cut those squares in half twice to create 88 triangles.
- 44—3⅞" squares from brown with blue floral for star background. Cut squares once in half diagonally to create 88 triangles.

For the first border, cut:
- 2—3½" x 60½" strips from brown with blue floral for top and bottom borders.
- 2—3½" x 84½" strips from brown with blue floral for side borders.

For the second border, cut:
- 2—3½" x 60½" strips from blue zig-zag print for top and bottom borders.
- 2—3½" x 84½" strips from blue zig-zag print for side borders.

For the third border, cut:
- 2—9½" x 84½" strips lengthwise from brown with blue geometric print for side borders.
- 2—6½" x 60½" strips lengthwise from brown with blue geometric print for top and bottom borders.
- 4—3½" x 12½" rectangles from brown with blue geometric print for border cornerstones.

For the binding, cut:

❖ 11—2½" strips the width of fabric from cream floral. Then piece together end to end.

SEWING INSTRUCTIONS

Use a ¼" seam allowance and sew fabrics right sides together. Press seams toward darker fabric.

Snowball block

1. Draw a diagonal line from corner to corner on the wrong side of 4—3½" brown with blue floral squares. With right sides together, place each of the marked squares on top of each corner of a 12½" cream floral square. Stitch on the marked lines and trim a ¼" seam allowance.

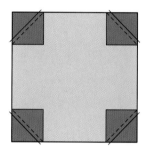

2. Press triangles open to complete one 12½" x 12½" block. Repeat to make a total of seventeen blocks.

Star block: Center unit

1. Sew 2 rust circular print triangles to opposite sides of a 4¾" blue with rust geometric print square. Press seams toward the triangles. Then sew 2 rust circular print triangles to the remaining sides of the 4¾" blue with rust geometric print square.

2. Trim the square, leaving a ¼" seam allowance beyond the points of the central blue with rust geometric print square. It should be 6½" x 6½". Repeat to make a total of 22 units.

Star block: Side unit

❖ Sew 2 blue with rust floral triangles to each short side of larger brown with blue floral triangles. Press seams toward the blue triangles and trim. The unit should measure 3½" x 6½". Repeat to make a total of 88 units.

Star block: Corner unit

❖ Sew a rust circular triangle to a brown with blue floral triangle to create a half-square triangle unit. Repeat to make a total of 88 of these units.

Columbine Clusters

Star block: Assembling the units

1. Referring to the 2nd row in diagram below, sew a side unit to opposite ends of a center unit. Press seams toward the side units. Repeat to make a total of 22 rows.

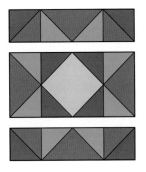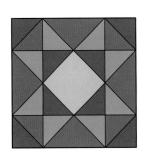

2. Referring to the top and bottom rows in the previous diagram, sew a corner unit to opposite sides of a side unit. Press seams toward the side units. Repeat to make a total of 44.
3. Referring to the previous diagram, sew together the rows from Steps 1 and 2 to create a 12½" x 12½" block.
4. Repeat Steps 1—3 to make a total of 22 Variable Star blocks (18 in the quilt center and 4 in the outer border corners).

Quilt center

1. Sew the Snowball and Variable Star blocks together, alternating each design to create 7 rows of five blocks each. Press seams in opposite directions. Make 3 rows like the first diagram and 4 rows like the second diagram.

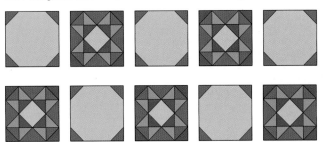

2. Referring to the quilt assembly diagram on page 83, sew the rows together to complete the 60½" x 84½" quilt center.

Borders

1. Sew a 3½" x 84½" blue zig-zag print lengthwise between a 3½" x 84½" brown with blue floral strip and a 9½" x 84½" brown with blue geometric strip to make a side border unit. Repeat to make a second side border unit. Then stitch the two finished border units to the long sides of the quilt.

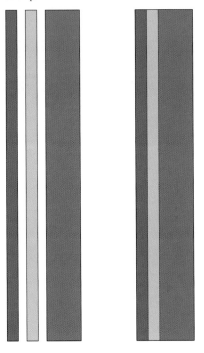

2. Sew a 3½" x 60½" blue zig-zag print lengthwise between a 3½" x 60½" brown with blue floral strip and a 6½" x 60½" brown with blue geometric strip. Repeat to make a second top/bottom border unit.

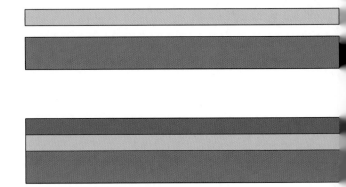

3. Sew a 3½" x 12½" brown with blue geometric rectangle to one side of each of the four Variable Star blocks that you reserved for the outer border cornerstones earlier.

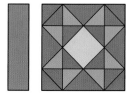

4. Referring to the quilt assembly diagram below, sew a unit from Step 3 to each end of the border strips created in Step 2.
5. Referring to the quilt assembly diagram below, sew the border strips created in Step 4 to the top and bottom of the quilt center.
6. Quilt, bind, and enjoy.

Assembly Diagram

Appliqué Quilts

You needn't always rely on the typical palette of quilting cottons to create enchanting appliqué quilts. Add some unexpected fabrics to the mix. Although it evokes the classic charm of early 19th-century medallion-style quilts, Karen's Gigi's Quilt puts a twist on tradition with black silk homespun fabric. It creates a dramatic backdrop for appliqué in the central block and reappears in the pieced blocks. Rather than hand appliquéing her creation as quilters of the 19th century would have done, Karen opted for speedier raw-edge machine appliqué.

Like her mother, Erin thought outside the box for her creative Shoe Fantasy quilt. Instead of the typical 100% cotton fabric, she gathered fashionable fabrics such as rayon/cotton blend and faux leather from the aisles of decorator textile shops, then prowled the craft stores for glittery embellishments. The shiny silver chains, crystals, and feathers that adorn her quilt are just her style—young and trendy!

Gigi's Quilt

Designed by Karen Witt • Finished quilt size: 38" x 44"

❧

The cheerful tulips of this quilt reminded me of April in Paris, so of course it had
to be named Gigi's Quilt! Inspired by the 1820s medallion-style quilts, this project
comes together fairly quickly—thanks to its compact size and wide borders. Combining pieced
and appliqué blocks, I stepped outside the typical palette of quilting fabrics by mixing silk homespun fabric
with traditional quilting cottons. Try adding heavier weight fabrics such as Osnaburg and linen to your quilts.
Do keep in mind that these fabrics won't stand up to frequent laundering. The homespun silk I used in this
quilt, for example, is washable but it will lose its sheen and become limp after repeated launderings. An oc-
casional trip to the dryer on the "fluff" setting will eliminate the need for frequent laundering.

FABRIC REQUIREMENTS

**Center appliqué block and 4
corner blocks:**

- 1—22" x 22" square black silk
  homespun for center block background and 4 corner block borders
- Fat quarter green print for leaves
  in center appliqué block
  and 2 pieced star blocks
- Fat eighth rust tonal for tulip centers in center appliqué block
  and 2 pieced star blocks
- 1—5" x 12" piece coral print for
  tulips in center appliqué block
- 1—5" x 5" square gold tonal for
  vase in center appliqué block

**2 appliqué corner blocks, outer
border, and binding:**

- 1 yard large-scale floral or chintz

**1st and 3rd borders and four corner
block backgrounds:**

- ½ yard beige print

2nd border:

- ⅔ yard striped border print

CUTTING INSTRUCTIONS

Measurements include a ¼" seam allowance unless otherwise noted. **All
templates for this project do not include seam allowances.** You will need to
reverse directional templates if doing the fusible web appliqué method that I
used. Trace appliqué templates onto the paper side of fusible web, leaving at
least a ½" between shapes. Roughly cut them out. Following manufacturer's
instructions, fuse the web onto the wrong side of the fabrics. Carefully cut out
the templates and remove the paper backing.

For center appliqué block, cut:

- 1—13" x 19" rectangle from black silk homespun for center background.
- 3 tulip templates on page 94 from coral print.
- 3 tulip center templates on page 94 from rust tonal.
- 3 leaf templates on page 93 from green print.
- 1 vase template on page 93 from gold tonal. (This template should be cut so
  that the black silk homespun fabric will show underneath.)

For 2 appliqué corner blocks, cut:

- 8 melon templates on page 93 from large-scale floral or chintz.
- 2—7" squares from beige print for backgrounds.
- 4—1" x 6½" rectangles from black silk homespun.
- 4—1" x 7½" rectangles from black silk homespun.

For 2 pieced corner blocks, cut:

- 2—2¾" squares from rust tonal. Then cut each square in half twice diagonally to make 8 "B" triangles.
- 16—2" squares from rust tonal.

- 4—2⅜" squares from green print. Then cut each square once in half diagonally to make 8 "C" triangles.

- 2—2¾" squares from beige print. Then cut each square twice in half diagonally to make 8 "A" triangles.

- 8—2" x 3½" rectangles from beige print.
- 8—2" squares from beige print.
- 4—1" x 6½" rectangles from black silk homespun for border strips.
- 4—1" x 7½" rectangles from black silk homespun for border strips.

For first border, cut:
- 2—1½" x 12½" strips from beige print for top and bottom borders.
- 2—1½" x 20½" strips from beige print for side borders.

For second border, fussy cut:
- 2—7½" x 14½" strips lengthwise from striped border print for top and bottom borders.
- 2—7½" x 20½" strips from striped border print for side borders.

For third border, cut:
- 2—1½" x 28½" strips from beige print for top and bottom borders.
- 2—1½" x 36½" strips from beige print for side borders.

For outer border, cut:
- 2—4½" x 36½" strips from floral/chintz print for side borders.
- 2—4½" x 38½" strips from floral/chintz print for top and bottom borders.

For binding, cut:
- 4—2 ¼" strips the width of floral/chintz fabric. Sew pieces together end to end.

SEWING INSTRUCTIONS

Use a ¼" seam allowance and sew all fabrics right sides together. Press seams toward darker fabric.

Center appliqué block

1. To stabilize your block for appliquéing later, heavily starch the back side of your background fabric. Press the 13" x 19" black silk homespun appliqué background rectangle into quarters. Mark the center. Referring to the diagram below for placement, arrange the tulips, tulip centers, stems/leaves, and vase on the black silk homespun. Fuse them in place.

2. Using matching thread, machine appliqué around the raw edges of each appliqué shape. Trim the black silk homespun background rectangle to 12½" x 18½". The piece was initially cut larger because machine appliqué tends to cause the background fabric to pucker and pull, resulting in a smaller piece than you started with.

Pieced block: Center section

1. Sew a beige print "A" triangle to a rust tonal "B" triangle. It is important that the rust triangle be to the left and the cream to the right. Repeat to make a total of 8 units.

2. Sew the unit created in Step 1 to a green print "C" triangle. Press and trim the block to 2" square. Make a total of 8 of these units.

3. Sew four units created in Step 2 to make one unit. Repeat to make a second unit.

Pieced block: Side section

1. Draw a diagonal line on the wrong side of a 2" rust print square. With right sides together, layer the marked square on top of a 2" x 3½" beige print rectangle. Be careful to orient the drawn lines as shown below.

2. Stitch on the drawn line. Then trim a ¼" seam allowance from the stitched line.

3. Press the triangle open. On the opposite side of the 2" x 3½" beige print rectangle, layer a marked 2" rust print square with right sides together. Be careful to orient the drawn lines as shown below.

4. Stitch on the drawn line.

5. Then trim a ¼" seam allowance from the stitched line. Press the triangle open. This completes the side section unit.

6. Repeat Steps 1-5 to create a total of 8 side section units.

Pieced block: Assembling the block

1. Referring to the middle row in diagram below, sew a side section to opposite sides of a center section. Repeat to create 2 of these rows.

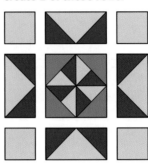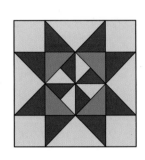

2. Referring to the top and bottom rows in the previous diagram, sew a 2" beige print square to opposite ends of a side section. Repeat to create a total of 4 of these rows.

3. Referring to the previous diagram, sew two rows created in Step 2 to the top and bottom of one row created in Step 1 to make a 6½" x 6½" pieced corner block. Repeat to make a second block.

4. Sew 1—1" x 6½" black silk homespun strip to each side of the 2 pieced corner blocks. Then sew 1—1" x 7½" black silk homespun strip to the top and bottom of the 2 pieced corner blocks.

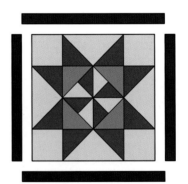

Appliquéd block

1. Press the 2—7" beige print background squares into quarters and mark the center.
2. Referring to the diagram below, arrange 4 melon pieces cut from the template on page 93 on each 7" beige print square. Then fuse in place.

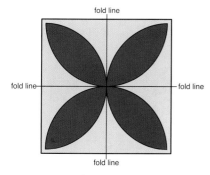

fold line

3. Using a matching thread, machine appliqué the raw edges of each appliqué shape. Repeat to make a total of 2 appliquéd corner blocks. Trim each block to 6½" square.
4. Sew 1—1" x 6½" black silk homespun strip to each side of the 2—6½" beige print appliqué corner blocks. Then sew 1—1" x 7½" black silk homespun strip to the top and bottom of the 2—6½" beige print appliqué corner blocks. Press seams. The block should measure 7½" x 7½".

ASSEMBLING THE BORDERS
First border

1. Referring to the quilt assembly diagram on page 92, sew the 2—1½" x 12½" beige print strips to the top and bottom of the center appliqué block.
2. Referring to the quilt assembly diagram on page 92, sew the 2—1½" x 20½" beige print strips to the sides of the center appliqué block.

Second border

1. Referring to the quilt assembly diagram on page 92, sew the 2—7½" x 20½" striped border print strips to both sides of the quilt center.
2. Referring to the assembly diagram on page 92, sew 1 pieced star block on one end of a 7½" x 14½" striped border print strip. Sew 1 appliquéd melon block on the other end of the strip. Repeat to make a second border strip. **Note that the positions of the pieced and appliqué blocks are switched in the top and bottom border strips.**
3. Referring to the assembly diagram on page 92, sew the two border strips created in Step 2 to the top and bottom of the quilt center.

Third border

1. Referring to the quilt assembly diagram on page 92, sew the 2—1½" x 28½" beige print strips to the top and bottom of the quilt center.
2. Referring to the quilt assembly diagram on page 92, sew the 2—1½" x 36½" beige print strips to both sides of the quilt center.

Outer border

1. Referring to the quilt assembly diagram on page 92, sew the 2—4½" x 36½" floral/chintz strips to both sides of the quilt center.
2. Referring to the quilt assembly diagram on page 92, sew the 2—4½" x 38½" floral/chintz strips to the top and bottom of the quilt center.

Quilt, bind, and enjoy. See the batting, quilting, and binding sections of the Barrington Medallion quilt on page 53 for period-appropriate finishes.

Gigi's Quilt

Assembly Diagram

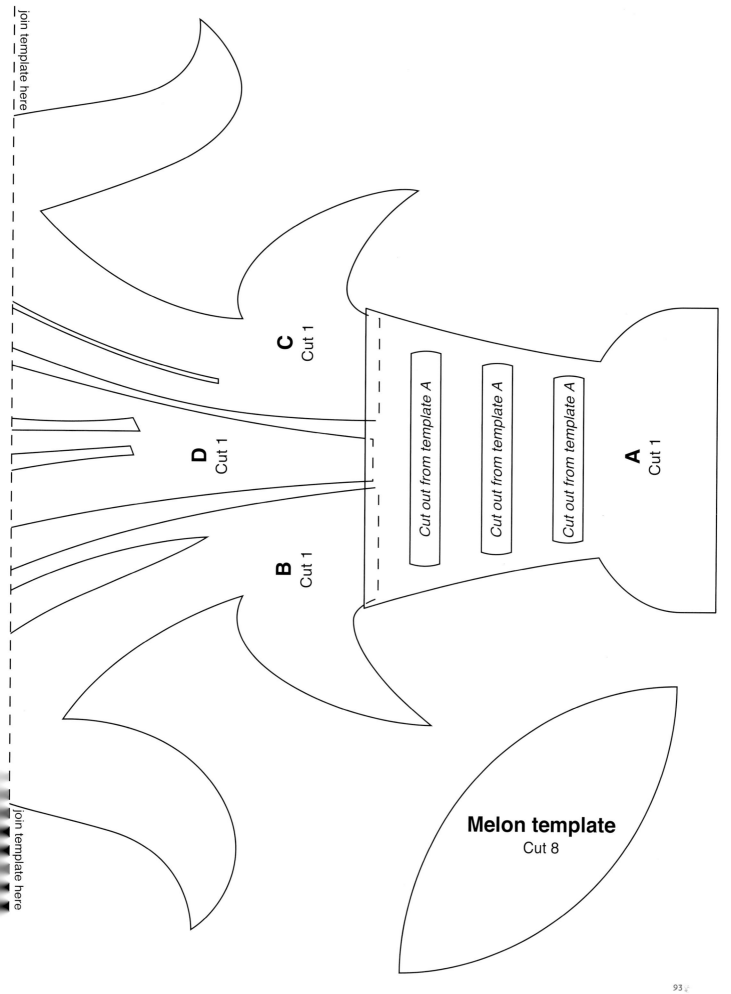

join template here

join template here

C
Cut 1

D
Cut 1

B
Cut 1

Cut out from template A

Cut out from template A

Cut out from template A

A
Cut 1

Melon template
Cut 8

Gigi's Quilt

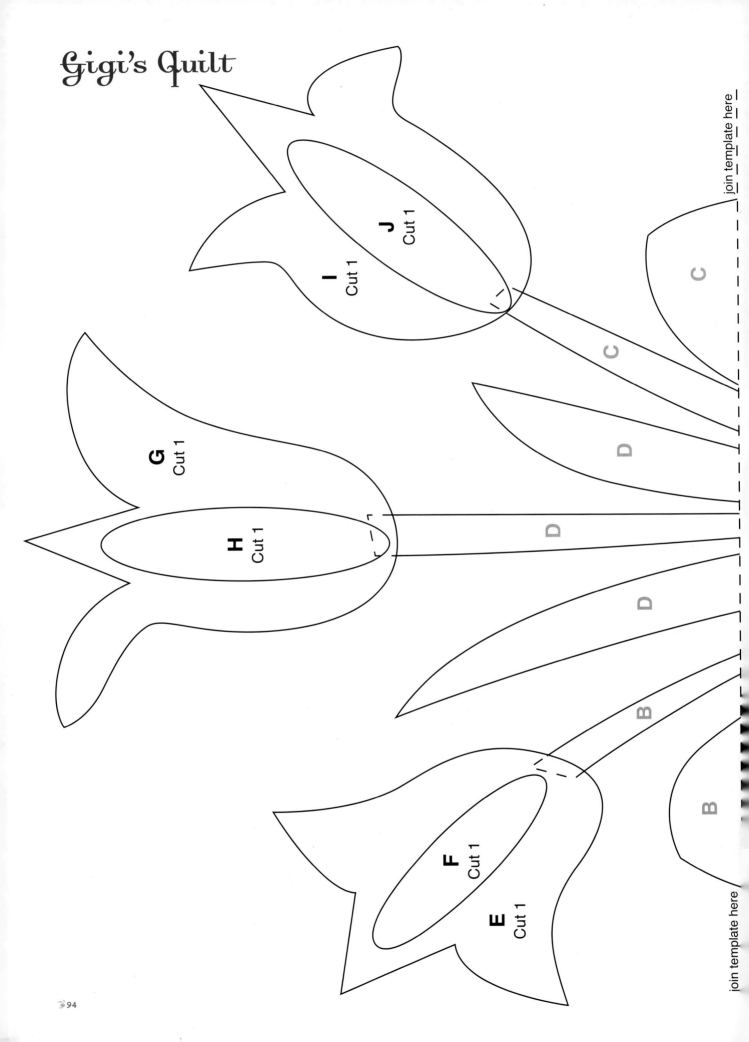

I
Cut 1

J
Cut 1

G
Cut 1

H
Cut 1

C

C

D

D

D

B

B

E
Cut 1

F
Cut 1

Shoe Fantasy

Designed by Erin Witt

Finished quilt size: 26" x 72"

Finished block size: 18"

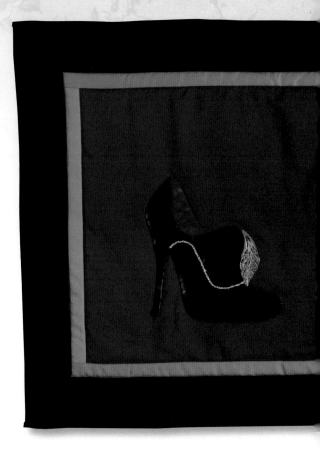

I have a confession to make. I am obsessed with shoes—not the sensible kind that are gentle on the feet and back—but the not-so-practical 4" stiletto type. There's just something about a pair of high heels that puts a swagger of confidence in my strut and a smile on my face. After all, unlike my favorite pair of skinny jeans or my slinky little black dress, my shoes never judge me after a weekend-long carb fest. This appliquéd wall hanging pays homage to several of my recent acquisitions. When it comes to shoes, I truly do believe variety is the spice of life!

FABRIC REQUIREMENTS

Blocks:

- 1⅛ yard royal blue rayon/cotton blend solid
- Fat quarter black textured faux leather solid for shoes
- Fat quarter camel faux leather for shoes
- Fat quarter batik for shoe linings

Individual block borders:

- ⅓ yard green rayon/cotton blend solid

Border, binding, and sleeve:

- 2½ yards black rayon/cotton blend solid for non pieced border seams OR 1⅛ yards for pieced border seams

(continued on next page)

CUTTING INSTRUCTIONS

All measurements include a ¼" seam allowance unless otherwise noted. The templates do not include seam allowances.

All appliqué templates will need to be reversed if using a fusible appliqué method. Trace templates onto the paper side of fusible web. Then cut around templates, leaving about a ½" between each piece. Fuse to the wrong side of fabric. Then cut out on traced lines.

For block backgrounds, cut:
- 3—20" squares from royal blue cotton/rayon solid.

For left shoe block, cut:
- Templates A, B, and D on page 102 from black textured faux leather solid.
- Template C on page 102 from batik.

For center shoe block, cut:
- Templates E, G, I, and J on pages 103 and 104 from camel faux leather solid.
- Templates F, H, L, and K on pages 103 and 104 from black faux leather solid.
- Templates M and N on pages 103 and 104 from batik.

For right shoe block, cut:
- Templates O, P, and Q on page 105 from black textured faux leather solid.
- Template R on page 105 from batik.

Fashion Forward

You can use 100% cotton fabric to make Shoe Fantasy—or step outside the box as I did and try designer and decorator fabrics such as satin, faux leather, and animal prints.

FABRIC REQUIREMENTS CONTINUED

- Lightweight fusible web if using cotton fabrics (Use heavyweight fusible web if using faux leather)
- Heavy-duty fabric glue
- Assorted embellishments to decorate shoes (I used 2 peacock feathers, a rhinestone-studded chain, thin black nylon rope, silver chain, and a flat silver pendant)
- Black pigma pen for marking left shoe lining in center shoe block

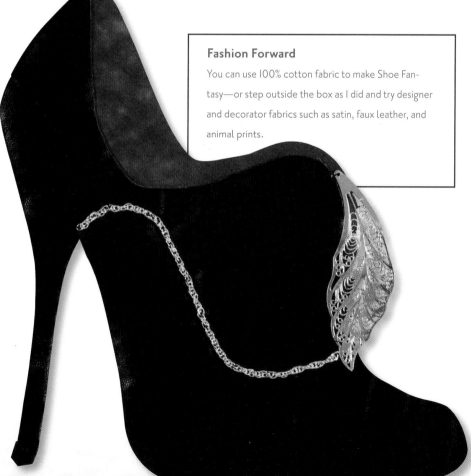

For block borders, cut:

- 6—1½" x 18½" strips from green cotton/rayon solid for side borders.
- 6—1½" x 20½" strips from green cotton/rayon solid for top and bottom borders.

For sashing and outer border, cut:

- 4—3½" x 20½" strips from black cotton/rayon solid for sashing between blocks.
- 2—3¼" x 20½" strips from black cotton/rayon solid for sashing at ends of blocks.
- 2—3¼" x 72" strips lengthwise from black cotton/rayon solid for top and bottom borders.

For sleeve (to hang the quilt), cut:

- 1—8½" x 72" strip lengthwise from black cotton/rayon solid.

For binding, cut:

- 2—2½" x 26" strips lengthwise.
- 2—2½" x 73" strips lengthwise.

SEWING INSTRUCTIONS

Use a ¼" seam allowance and sew fabrics right sides together except for appliqué pieces. Press seams toward darker fabric.

Appliqué the blocks

1. Referring to the diagrams below, arrange appliqué shapes on the three royal blue background squares. Then fuse. It may be necessary to secure the faux leather pieces with fabric glue. To accent the lining of the left shoe in the center, refer to the template on page 103 and draw a line with a black Pigma pen on the batik fabric.

2. Because I chose faux leather for all of my appliqué pieces, I used a fusible web and heavy-duty fabric glue to secure my fabric pieces to the background fabrics. If using traditional cotton fabrics, appliqué the pieces to the blocks using the appliqué technique of your choice. Then trim each royal blue block to 18½" x 18½".

Assembling the quilt

1. Sew the 2—1½" x 18½" strips from green cotton/rayon solid to both sides of each block.

2. Referring to the diagram above, sew the 2—1½" x 20½" strips from green cotton/rayon solid to the top and bottom of each block.
3. Sew the 2—3½" x 20½" black cotton/rayon solid sashing strips between each of the 3 blocks.

4. Referring to the assembly diagram on page 100, sew the 2—3¼" x 20½" black cotton/rayon solid strips to each end of the row created in Step 3.
5. Referring to the assembly diagram on page 100, sew the 2—3¼" x 72" black cotton/rayon solid strips to the top and bottom of the row created in Step 4. The quilt should now measure 26" x 72".

QUILTING THE QUILT

I quilted around the appliquéd shoes in each block to give them a 3-D appearance, then stitched in the ditch between the blocks, sashing, and borders.

Shoe Fantasy

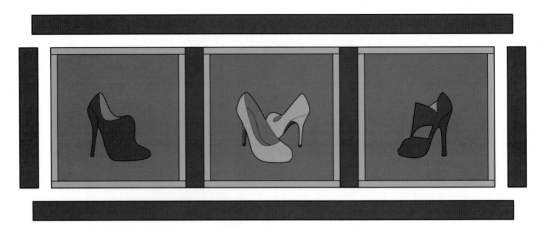

Assembly Diagram

SEWING THE BINDING AND SLEEVE

Since there are no diagonal design elements in this quilt, I thought a binding with butted ends would be most appropriate. I also needed a sleeve for hanging the quilt. Follow this easy technique to create both in tandem.

1. Fold under the short side edges of the 8½" x 72" sleeve a ¼". Then fold them under again another ¼" to enclose raw edges. Press and hem the folds.

2. Wrong sides together, fold the strip lengthwise, aligning the raw edges. Press. Then set aside.

3. Sew one 2½" x 26" binding strip to each side of the quilt.

4. Sew one 2½" x 73" binding strip to the top and bottom of the quilt, leaving a ¼" of excess binding at each corner.

5. Center the folded sleeve strip created in Steps 1-2 along the top edge of the quilt against the backing, aligning its raw edges with the edges of the quilt. Sew along the entire length of the sleeve ⅜" from the raw edge.

6. At the corners, tuck raw edges inside the binding strips, trimming excess binding fabric if necessary to reduce bulk.

7. Roll the binding to the back side of the quilt and whip-stitch it in place along the top, bottom and side edges.

8. To allow room for a hanging rod, use a water-soluble marker to draw a line on the quilt backing 3¾" from the top of the binding. Whipstitch the lower edge of the sleeve in place, using the drawn line as a guide and catching the backing and batting of the quilt with your stitches.

EMBELLISHING THE QUILT

Resist the temptation to embellish the shoes until the quilt is finished. Shifting the quilt as it is quilted and bound may cause the embellishments to come loose. Attach the embellishments as desired and secure them with needle and thread. I dressed up the left shoe block with a silver-braided chain and a shiny large silver pendant. On the center block, I accentuated the heels with peacock feathers and outlined the shoe tops with a thin black nylon rope. The shoe on the right is adorned with rows of rhinestone-studded chain. If using faux leather, you will need to use a leather needle to sew through the shoe when attaching embellishments.

> **Tip**
>
> Faux leathers are heavy and may eventually come loose from the quilt. If they do, simply apply a small quantity of heavy-duty fabric glue with a toothpick to refasten any loose edges. Weigh it down with a stack of heavy books until the glue dries.

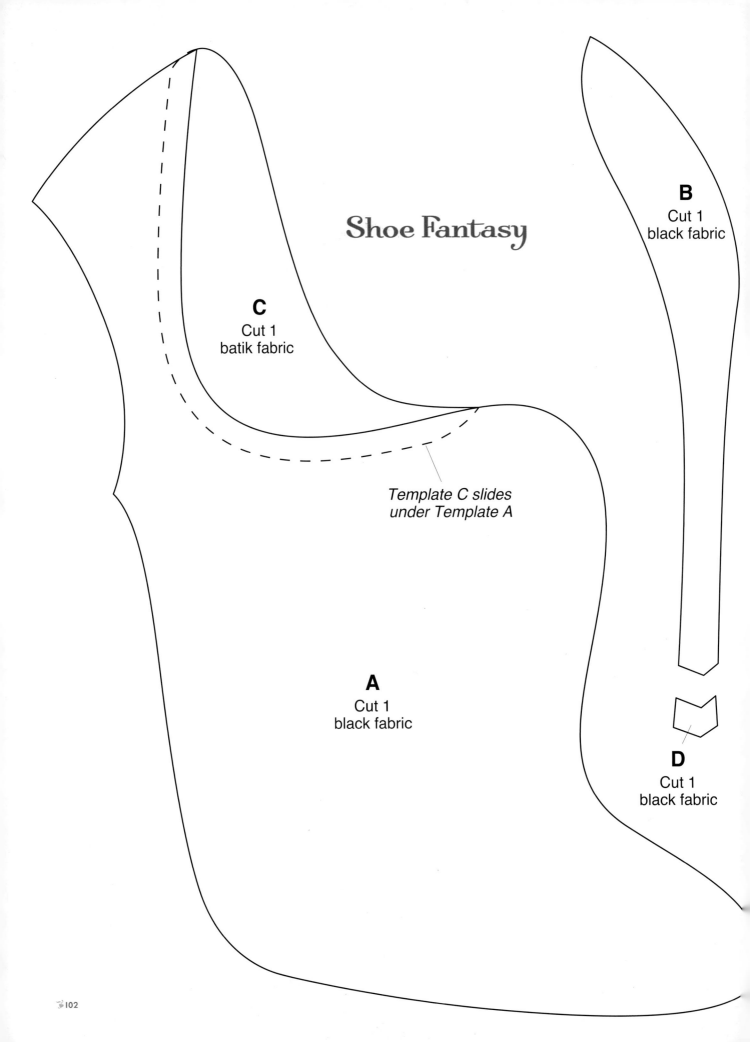

Shoe Fantasy

C
Cut 1
batik fabric

B
Cut 1
black fabric

*Template C slides
under Template A*

A
Cut 1
black fabric

D
Cut 1
black fabric

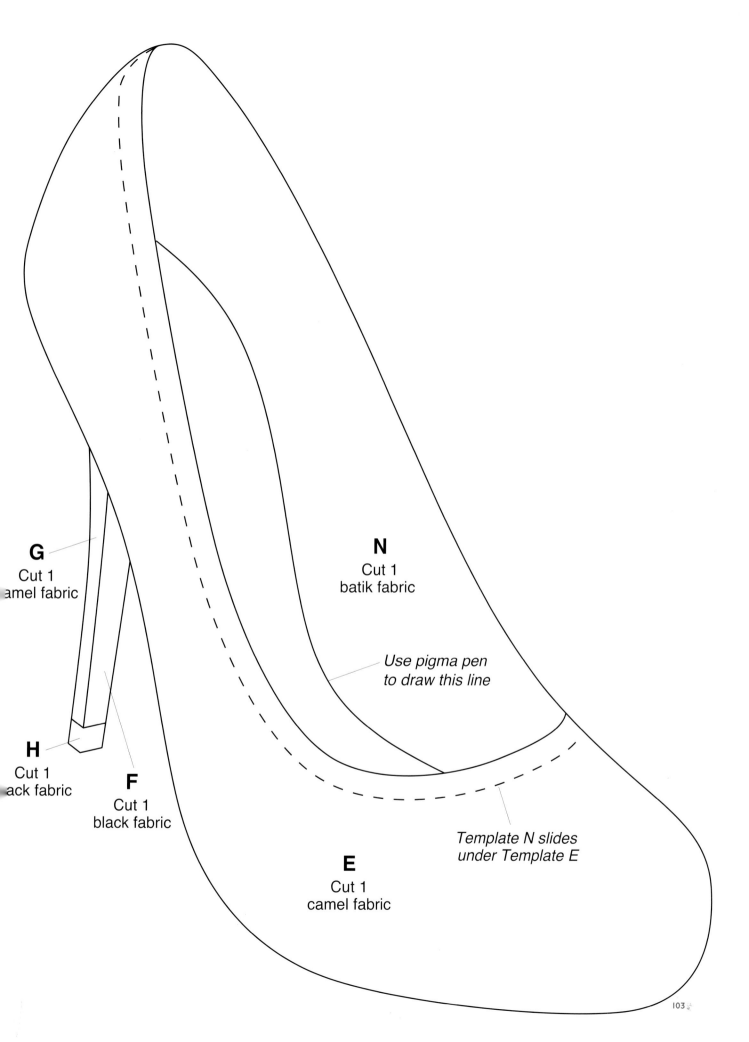

G
Cut 1
camel fabric

H
Cut 1
black fabric

F
Cut 1
black fabric

N
Cut 1
batik fabric

*Use pigma pen
to draw this line*

*Template N slides
under Template E*

E
Cut 1
camel fabric

Shoe Fantasy

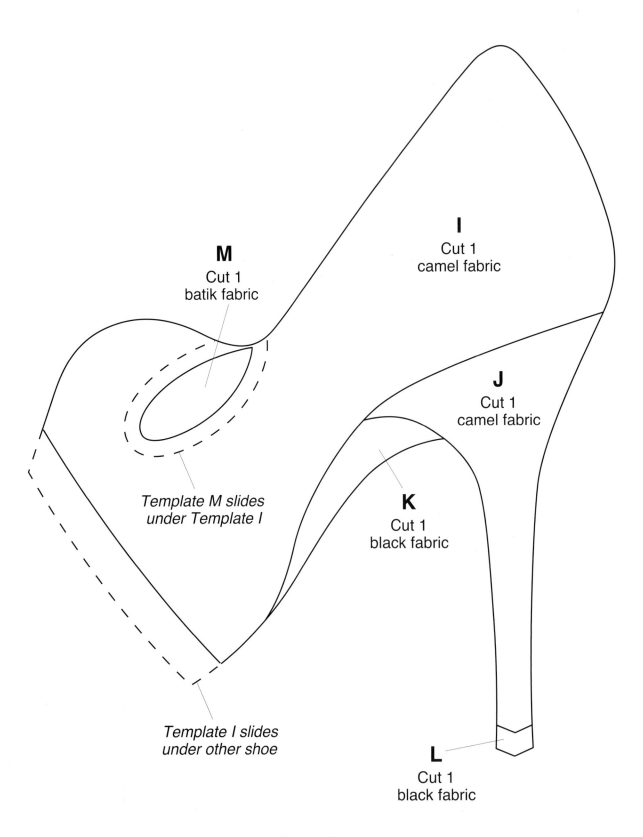

M
Cut 1
batik fabric

I
Cut 1
camel fabric

J
Cut 1
camel fabric

*Template M slides
under Template I*

K
Cut 1
black fabric

*Template I slides
under other shoe*

L
Cut 1
black fabric

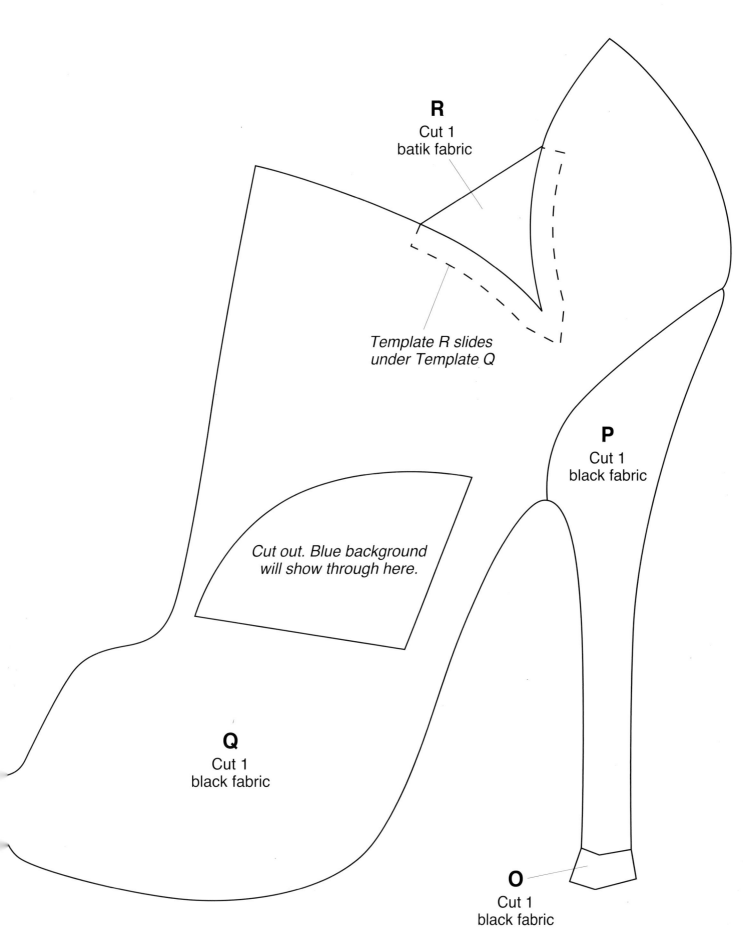

R
Cut 1
batik fabric

*Template R slides
under Template Q*

P
Cut 1
black fabric

*Cut out. Blue background
will show through here.*

Q
Cut 1
black fabric

O
Cut 1
black fabric

Tree of Life Medallion Quilt
2001

Inspired by Indian Palampores
and Medallion Quilts of the early 1800's

Designed and Constructed by Karen Witt
Winchester, Kentucky

Quilted by Karen Witt and the Belmont Church
Quilters, Winchester, Kentucky

Civil War Sampler
2000-2002

Designed and Constructed by Karen Witt
Winchester, KY

Quilted by Karen Witt and
Minnie Prater ~ Wallingford, KY

Don't Forget the Label

You've completed your quilt and now it's ready to display in your home or give as a gift, right? Not quite! Every quilt needs a label so that future generations will know the history behind your quilt. When Karen's mother died, we found a box with several silver thimbles in her house. One was labeled simply, "Grandmother Alley," Karen's great grandmother and Erin's great-great grandmother. What a find! And all because of a very simple label.

In theory, we all understand the importance of labeling our quilts and we all have good intentions of making them. In fact, perhaps the most common reason our quilts don't have labels is that we want to make special ones but can't quite figure out how to create them. Fancy labels are wonderful but simple ones can also capture your quilt's story.

According to quilt historians, every quilt should have at least three essential pieces of information: your full name, including maiden name (If you're divorced, consider adding that name as well, especially if your children have that last name); the city and state where you lived when you finished the quilt; and the date the quilt was completed. Additional information you might want to include is the quilt's name, your source of inspiration, and the names and locations of other people who worked on it.

Label Tips

— ⚜ —

KAREN'S LABEL TIPS

As quilt appraisers will attest, the provenance of an antique quilt is key to its value. And a signature is an important part of that provenance. It is as important as an artist signing his or her portrait. Like a painting, a quilt is a unique reflection of its creator that deserves to be recorded for posterity. I keep recipe cards and letters that were handwritten by my mother and grandmother, and just seeing the distinct curves and swirls of their penmanship brings back so many pleasant memories.

Recording the provenance of your quilt needn't be time-consuming. In fact, you don't even have to create a separate piece of fabric for a label. Even a simple signature with all the essential details written on the quilt backing can be sufficient. Be sure to write the details with a fabric-safe pen and press the inked area with an iron to set the ink.

For a decorative, easy-to-create flourish, use a rubber signature stamp specifically designed for quilts. Stamps like the one pictured on page 109 are authentic reproductions of the type of signature stamps that quilters of the mid 1800s used to sign their album-style blocks. For best results when working with signature stamps, first back the fabric with freezer paper to stabilize the surface for writing. Iron the waxy side of the freezer paper to the back side of your fabric against a hard surface before applying the stamped image. For small areas, you can use a 2-inch piece of masking tape or painter's tape in place of the freezer paper.

Signature stamps also work great for special blocks that you made on a particularly memorable date such as your birthday or anniversary. Stamping the fabric and recording the month, day, and year will capture that special piece of personal history for years to come.

Sometimes a quilt calls for a special label. I designed, hand pieced, and hand quilted a Civil War Sampler quilt and Tree of Life quilt and wanted unique pieced labels to document them (see photo on page 106). For my labels, I reduced the size of the pieced blocks featured in the quilts and recorded all the essential identification in a center area, including the names of others who worked on the projects. A light box is especially handy when positioning the words onto the fabric. After I appliquéd the label in place, I quilted through the batting (but not the front) so the label looks like a permanent part of the quilt.

I took a similar approach with my Barrington Medallion quilt label, shown above, by repeating a design motif from the quilt top. To make the label, simply adapt a section of the stair-step motif from the border pattern and appliqué it to a 6½" square piece of fabric. If you want to make it even fancier, add narrow piping to the outside edge as shown in the photo.

Above, inset: For her Barrington Medallion quilt label, Karen repeated a design element from the quilt top.

On this page, above and left: Designed specifically for quiltmaking, reproductions of authentic historical signature stamps make fitting labels for 1800s-style quilts. These signature stamps are available from Reproduction Quilts. To order, log on to www.reproductionquilts.com or call 859/333-6232.

Label Tips

ERIN'S LABEL TIPS

I like to let the personality of my quilt dictate the type of label I make. For example, the bright and cheerful color palette of my College Bound quilt called for an equally lighthearted label. Designing the perfect label can be a creative experience and it is a great way to incorporate your other hobbies. If you enjoy scrapbooking and rubber stamping, you're probably already familiar with fabric-safe ink and Pigma pens. When heat set, these inks will hold up to daily use and laundering. While there are stamps specifically designed for quilting, you can use practically any crafting rubber stamp to decorate your quilt labels.

I embellished my College Bound label, shown above, with images from a rubber stamp collection that I typically use to make invitations for children's special occasions. I accented the stamped designs with dashes of color from a Pigma pen. To create the writing on the label, I simply formatted the text on the computer, printed it out, then laid a sheet of ruled paper beneath the stamped fabric label so I could easily fill in the rest of the important details in my own handwriting. This handy method eliminates the pressure of centering and spacing the words as well as the risk of running out of space.

For my Southern Belle quilt, I created a label, shown above, that incorporated my love of photography with a photo of the quilt. I often use photo transfer paper-backed fabric to make computerized labels featuring a digital image of the quilt as well as all the essentials mentioned on page 107. I usually try to take the photo of the quilt in the room in which it resides—another personalized touch! Another fun idea is to have a photo taken of you working on that specific quilt. This is especially nice if you're giving the quilt as a gift. Just think of how much the recipient will treasure such a personalized reminder of the quiltmaker!